Yes!

And...

LEADERSHIP LESSONS FROM THE WORLD OF IMPROVISATION

D0720972

Amy Lisewski

"Organizations come into being primarily because groups of aligned people – teams – have the ability to accomplish exponentially greater outcomes than the work output of individuals. **Teaming and team building are a pervasive focus of any leader.**" – Eric Kaufmann

"Yes! And…" – The Second City (and every improviser since)

Are the people of your organization aligned to accomplish extraordinary results as a team?

List 3 things you have done in the past quarter to connect your team and improve their ability to collaborate and work towards a common vision.

_____

_____

_____

Let's put the principles and practices of improv to work to:

CONNECT + COMMUNICATE
+ COLLABORATE

Innovation Challenge

Each of you works for the "Impossible Mission Task Force." One of you is the CEO. The Rubber Band Company of the World has just learned that a company has developed a product that will make rubber bands as we know them obsolete. In order to survive, you need to develop new practical uses for rubber bands. Each group has 5 minutes to generate as many ideas for uses of the rubber band. At the end of 5 minutes I am going to ask the CEO to pitch me (the client).

D.O.V.E.

Don't judge

Outrageous ideas are desirable

Volume & Variety

Extend and Elaborate

Debrief

- In what ways if any did your inner critic affect your participation?

- Did you notice any changes in your thinking as the game progressed?

- How did working with the group enhance your ability to problem solve?

- How did it feel to "Yes! And…"?

- How did your leader/CEO do? What did they do well?

- How can you apply what you experienced in this game to ideation or problem solving in your company?

List 3 more ways that you, as a leader, can develop a stronger culture of support, trust, communication, and collaboration in your organization.

_____

_____

_____

HIGHLY ENGAGING & RESULTS-FOCUSED PROFESSIONAL DEVELOPMENT

As featured in

"We received rave reviews from our tribe members (employees) and created a significant shift in our mindset as it relates to positive communication."

Joanne Lamb, WD-40

"FCI directly related all their lessons to our GoPro brand, and through the magic of improvisation we elevated our game."

Jeff Youel, GoPro

"We loved the variety of exercises to get us all working together. It was exactly what we needed!"

Tana Lorah, Kaiser Permanente

CONTACT

- **Highly-interactive and memorable keynote speaker. Invite me to your next retreat or conference.**

- **A virtual coaching package to help you implement the tools of today's lessons!**

- **Team building, communication, and collaboration workshops.**

- **Brainstorming and meeting facilitation.**

Amy Lisewski
(619) 306-6047
amy@finestcityimprov.com

Finest City Improv
4250 Louisiana St.
San Diego CA 92104

"Yes, but..."

You need 100 great ideas before lunch but all you get is a lot of "that won't work" or "we tried it before" responses. More often that not, people are willing to tell you why something won't work rather than why it just might!

Spirited collaboration means everyone is co-creating with a "Yes! And..." mindset just like we use in improvisation. Diverse opinions and ideas are welcomed and lead to unexpected improvements to products, services, or processes. What can you do as a leader to empower your team members to operate with a "Yes! And..." mindset?

GAMES PLAYED   OBSERVATIONS & APPLICATIONS

"The strength of the team is each individual member. The strength of each member is the team." - Phil Jackson

WHAT IS IMPROV?

Imagine you are standing on a stage with bright lights shining down on you... there's no set or props, no costumes, and no script. You look in front of you to see at least 50 people mere meters from you waiting to be entertained. You ask them to shout out a single word to inspire the show you will create on the spot. Your goal: the funniest theater they've ever seen.

Now also look to your right and your left, because right there with you are your teammates. They're right there in this high-pressure situation with you and one thing you know for sure is whatever happens...

THEY HAVE YOUR BACK.

HUMOR + RESULTS

READY

Step away from your desks, put on your comfy shoes, and take time to laugh and learn! For the next few hours it's team time! We'll need a room cleared of obstacles so we can stand and play some simple and fun games.

SET

Your facilitator will create a safe space for everyone to get comfortable and begin to play. They'll keep an eye on everyone's comfort level and adjust for each group. Fun and learning truly happens just outside our comfort zones.

ACTION

We'll play progressively more challenging games and exercises designed to match one of our three key programs or your specific goals. Your team takes their rekindled excitement and skills back to their day-to-day!

ADVANCE PRAISE

If you've been hungry to connect with your true calling but aren't sure how to start on that journey, this book should go straight to the top of your reading list. Amy showed me how to say "YES! And . . ." to all the good I had already created by helping heart-centered entrepreneurs sell their services without being salesy AND stay open to discovering my even bigger mission that is driving that. As Amy teaches . . . "always add!" And adding the teachings in this book to your success tool box is a winning move!"

Lisa Sasevich
Author of www.BoostYourSalesBook.com, The Invisible Close

Improvisation has so many applications beyond the art of immediate comic creation. Amy is a joyful badass* who practices what she preaches. She shares the precepts of improv that give you tools that can be easily applied to so many facets of your life. If joy in your personal and professional life is your ultimate goal, this book is for *you*.

Susan Messing
Improviser Bad Ass at Large
*because it takes one to know one

If you desire to create the life you are meant to live but aren't sure how to start on that journey, than this book should go straight to the top of your reading list."

JJ Virgin CNS, CHFS
Celebrity Nutrition & Fitness Expert
Author of the NYT bestsellers: *The Virgin Diet* & *Sugar Impact Diet*
www.jjvirgin.com

Relax, We're All Just Making This Stuff Up! is exactly what anyone who wants to be more authentic, vulnerable, captivating, courageous and charismatic needs in their toolbox. I first met Amy Lisewski and her improv troupe at a corporate training event. I was instantly pulled in and transfixed by the exercises, the energy, and the feeling I got from the experiences her team guided us through. I've hungered for the opportunity to give myself permission to completely let go, expand my comfort zone, and be willing to fail spectacularly and repeatedly wherever I speak, present, or am in a public space. I've been a public speaker for over a decade, speaking to audiences in the hundreds or thousands—and I need all the help I can get to constantly hone my skills and push to new levels and limits. Next stop for me is improv! I'm inspired to take things to the next step, and Amy can certainly inspire you, too!

Mike Koenigs
Serial Entrepreneur and 10-Time #1 Bestselling Author
www.YouEverywhereNow.com

Amy has built a wonderful improv community and theater in San Diego. Improv will make you better in all aspects of your life. You don't have to be an improviser to read this book. Start your own journey today by reading Amy's book, and start feeling the power of yes!

Nick Armstrong
Founder of Camp Improv Utopia and Co-Founder of The Improv Network

If you haven't yet had the good fortune to take an improv class, you're holding the next best thing right here in your hands. With wit, warmth, and an improviser's generosity of spirit, Amy

Lisewski shares inspiring stories and super-fun improv games that reveal the life-changing power of this amazing art form. *Relax!* will help you boost your confidence, unleash your creativity, enrich your personal and professional relationships, and fill your life with so much more—there is no better word for it—joy. Two enthusiastic thumbs up!

Martha Barnette
Host of the nationally syndicated public radio show *A Way with Words*

As leaders we are constantly called upon to speak to, present to, and influence others. Many of us get in our way by being overly anxious or self-conscious, or lacking the confidence to deliver our message with ease and spontaneity. With the use of exercises and some basic rules, Amy helps us unleash our creativity and bring more joy and fun into our lives and into the lives of those we impact.w

Ivy Gordon
Chair, Vistage International
www.ivygordon.com

Darn it. Amy has let the cat out of the bag and revealed all our *improvluscious* trade secrets in this book! Now *everyone* will have a guide for how to take more risks, strengthen their voices, conquer their fear of failure, work collaboratively, and rule the world. At least she didn't tell our biggest improv secret: Always be a pirate. Wait! Don't print that last part, Amy.

Pam Victor
Head of Happiness of Happier Valley Comedy
Co-author of *Improvisation at the Speed of Life: The TJ & Dave Book*

What a great opportunity to learn these principles of improv that Amy presents to help you flourish and realize what Shakespeare shared: All the world's a stage. If you're going to be fully engaged on the stage of life, you might as well learn some tips of the trade to excel in a life worth living. It is why I have been studying with Amy and Finest City Improv going onto three years.

My mentor and one of the seminal thinkers in communication, Lee Thayer, holds that "improv" techniques are one of the core competencies for being a uniquely effective leader. Improv is practical, pragmatic, and efficacious because leaders must continually improvise. They have to invent or create whatever role is required in never-to-be-repeated circumstances to make happen what ought to happen. Improv helps them in any situation to do what needs to be done to accomplish what needs to be accomplished. Leadership requires one to be prepared for any possible situation.

People forget that our lives are continually one improv scene after another. What better way to prepare oneself than learning improv? It helps one to be present, to listen, and to increase one's repertoire and capacity for living life fully.

In the various roles we play from parent, employee, co-worker and sibling to spouse, friend, or lover, we have to shift roles as the circumstances change from moment to moment. Being able to do that is a fundamental part of being competent and being able to deal with whatever comes at us. The measure of performance is: performance. What better way to prepare yourself to competently perform your roles in life than improv, so you can deal with the real improv: Your Life. What Amy shares is a great start.

Austin "Ozzie" Gontang, Ph.D.
Master Chair, Vistage International
Using the advantage of peers toward leadership virtuosity

Bottom line: Amy is inspirational. She teaches you to live your life like an improv scene—finding joy in every moment. If you have ever wondered whether you would enjoy taking an improvisation class and what you would get out of it personally, read this book.

Micah D. Parzen, Ph.D., J.D.
Chief Executive Officer
San Diego Museum of Man

In a world of leadership models and metrics, sometimes our best gift comes from embracing the unscripted. *Relax, We're All Just Making This Stuff Up!* offers a refreshing approach to generating rapid-fire, collaborative innovation, based on insights from learning and performing improv. Amy Lisewski augments her seven principles of improvisation with stories and exercises to build skills and expand thinking, confidence, and awareness. *Relax!* will enable leaders and their teams (aka ensembles) to tap the power of vulnerability, courage, authenticity, and unfettered creativity.

Dr. Kathryn Bingham
Chief Essentialist Officer & Executive Coach, LEADistics

RELAX, WE'RE ALL JUST MAKING THIS STUFF UP!

USING THE TOOLS OF
IMPROVISATION TO CULTIVATE MORE
COURAGE AND JOY IN YOUR LIFE

AMY LISEWSKI

Printed and bound in the United States of America
ISBN: 978-0-9977030-0-9
Library of Congress Control Number: 2016910211

ACKNOWLEDGEMENTS

Kat Brown for showing me what joy looks like every day and supporting me in finding mine. Jesse Suphan for being the greatest "pageant mom" Kat and I could ask for. Zoe Hayman for helping to kick-start the writing process. Mom and Dad for supporting me through as many "spectacular failures" as there were successes. Becca for always having my back. To all the teachers, supporters, fans, students, performers and friends of Finest City Improv. Yes! And . . .

DEDICATION

For Esme. Thank you for being in my ensemble.
And for all who graciously allowed me to share in their
lives and to share their stories in this book.

TABLE OF CONTENTS

If you cannot risk, you cannot grow. If you cannot grow,
you cannot become your best.
If you cannot become your best, you cannot be happy.
If you cannot be happy, what else matters?

—Dr. David Viscot ("Risking")

PREFACE

I was invited as a guest to attend an annual meeting of CEOs and key executives of San Diego companies. There were almost 600 people in the ballroom for the all-day meeting, featuring some of the top conference and business speakers. I knew only a couple of the people in the room and had only known them a very short time.

This was not my usual environment or scene. I have worked for various businesses over the past 20 years and had consulted with many, but I am not much for rooms full of suits and small talk. I was as confident as anyone else in the room to say hello, shake hands, and make polite introductions, but as an introvert I knew I would be exhausted by lunchtime. I was there to assess whether this organization would be useful for me in my career and to help expand my business. Since it was free, of course I said yes to the invitation. It was a great opportunity to network with many of the people in town who could become clients for my corporate improv business. I expected to exchange some business cards, have some brief and hopefully meaningful conversations, and go home with a few people I could email to introduce my services. I also planned to absorb anything I could from the speakers, whom I knew were some of the best on the speaking circuit.

What I did not expect was that I would inspire many in the room with a simple action that led to an important revelation: even the most successful people have trouble taking risks. However, if we don't take risks, we don't grow and find even greater happiness in our lives.

Happiness is essential to a life well-lived. When we put ourselves out on a limb in front of a crowd of people, we are risking our current happiness. If things go poorly (and we tend to expect that and judge it that way regardless of reality), we will spend the evening feeling miserable about ourselves and wishing we didn't look so foolish in front of others. Our happiness vanishes. To raise your hand and volunteer for an unknown task in front of hundreds of people takes immense courage. We assume it will lead to humiliation, or at least a few minutes of extreme uncomfortableness. So why risk it?

One of the (very expensive) speakers that day was an artist who makes a living inspiring others to reach their full potential. He was there to inspire the room of 600 highly successful leaders to take risks in order to obtain big rewards. As usual, I was sitting at the table right in front of the stage (another understandably rare behavior). The speaker took the stage with U2's "It's a Beautiful Day" blasting on the speakers and, in just a few minutes, created a portrait of Bono on a black canvas. The image slowly revealed itself from the black void as the painter, with great flair jousted at the canvas with his brush. Greatly impressed, the audience cheered.

When he finished the painting, he began the portion of his presentation in which he challenges the audience to look inward and see what untapped potential we are hiding within us. He referenced the TV program "Fear Factor" to build anxiety as he brought out a tennis ball and tossed it randomly to someone in the audience. He then put that person on the spot, asking if he was willing to step onto the stage and participate in a "Fear Factor"-type activity in front of all 600 people. He showed us a sealed envelope with the words "Fear Factor" written across it. The reaction from the man who caught the tennis ball was understandable. Visibly afraid, he was a like a deer in headlights or, literally, a person unexpectedly put in the spotlight.

We've all been in his shoes at some time to some degree. Our heart begins to beat faster, our stomach turns, our palms begin to sweat, and time seems to slow to a crawl as we notice everyone staring at us. It was fascinating to watch: everyone at his table physically pulled away from him, attempting to create as much distance as possible from the spotlight he was in. People at the surrounding tables craned their necks to get a glimpse of this poor soul and, by the sounds coming from around the room, everyone was relieved not to be holding the tennis ball. "And that's why you never sit near the front!" I could hear them all saying to themselves. As for me, I was disappointed that I didn't get to catch the tennis ball.

As the speaker invited this subject onstage, nervous laughter echoed throughout the ballroom. And then the speaker gave the man one chance to escape this predicament . . . find someone willing to take his place. My hand shot up immediately. The speaker noticed but kept focused on the unwilling "volunteer." I could tell he wanted to encourage him to take the stage rather than take the easy way out.

I don't think the speaker was used to someone so quickly offering to take the stage. As he joked about someone volunteering to take this man's spot, I sat there with my hand raised confidently, but inside I was pleading to have this opportunity. The man noticed me and looked immediately thrilled. "Yes! I will take your place!" I told him. The speaker then turned to me somewhat grudgingly as all eyes turned from the original "victim" to me. The look on everyone's face clearly communicated that I must be insane. I was a strange creature that somehow snuck into this room and did not belong among them. I looked around, and that's when I realized I was the *only* one in a room of almost 600 confident and successful people who had willingly volunteered to relieve this man of his suffering. To be honest, I wanted whatever undefined reward awaited whomever took that challenge.

So I went on stage and was asked to state my name into the microphone. Nailed it! Then the speaker handed me the envelope with the words "Fear Factor" written on it, and a mischievous grin erupted across his face. Inside was the activity I would be compelled to carry out in front the entire audience.

The speaker had intentionally built to this moment with great fanfare to achieve maximum effect, and had done an excellent job. I ripped the envelope open and read it aloud: "You are the proud owner of the painting." The sounds of distress in the room abruptly turned to ones of excitement and applause. As I looked out at the audience I thought, "Well, of course something good would come of this! Why wouldn't it?"

I had just won a valuable painting by simply raising my hand and agreeing to step on stage and take a risk. And I earned my reward with what I considered little effort. But almost 600 people saw it differently. After the presentation I was immediately approached by many in the room. They all asked me one thing: "How did you do that?!"

At first I looked at them slightly dumbfounded and replied, "Do what?"

"Raise your hand like that!" they exclaimed. That is the moment I realized that "Why not?" is not an easy response for most people.

Dozens of people shook my hand for the next hour and told me I was brave. In their eyes, I was very courageous for taking a chance and putting myself on the spot. I suppose I was. Many of them laughed and said, "Can you teach me how to do that?"

"To raise your hand when you are unsure of the outcome? Yes, in fact I can," I replied. "I teach improvisation!"

I'm not going to claim I don't care about looking foolish in front of others. I do. But until that day, I never realized just how much less I worry about that than most people. Or rather, I am more willing to risk my current and future happiness in hopes of potential reward. I am much more relaxed and open to these moments in life, which others see as courageous. I strive on stepping forward into the unknown in anticipation of undefined possibilities. The potential of "what if?" compels me more often than not to respond with, "Yes! why not?!" to whatever is presented to me. I'm relaxed and often excited because I know that we are all just making this stuff up as we go, anyway!

I went to the conference hoping to introduce myself to a few new connections and found an opportunity to be so memorable that dozens of people rushed to introduce themselves to me. I saw an opportunity to take the spotlight and immensely increase the potential for my goal that day. So, I leaped! I simply raised my hand and volunteered with no idea of the outcome—though I did know it had to be something "not that bad" and potentially awesome!

To be honest, I didn't particularly like the painting of Bono, and I'm not a fan of Bono, either (please don't throw this book away because I said that). I had no idea what I would do with the painting, but it was never about the painting anyway. It was about being offered the opportunity to be noticed by and introduced to 600 potential clients. Whatever reward the speaker had was simply a bonus.

Before I left, one attendee who was moved by the speaker's message and was a big fan of U2 asked if she could buy the painting from me. As I usually do, I immediately responded with "yes, why not?" She told me she not only loved the speaker and Bono but that she would always be reminded of my bravery in taking the stage as I did, something she wished she could do in her life.

She asked how much I wanted for the painting, and I told her to give me whatever it was worth to her. She wrote me a check for $500 on the spot. I realized I had just been *paid* $500 to attend a conference where I was given the opportunity to make a mark on almost 600 people I was hoping would become my clients.

Why did all this happen? It happened because I raised my hand and stepped into the undefined. I said "Yes!" to opportunity the second it presented itself, without the overwhelming fear of regret and unhappiness that might follow. That day I decided to figure out why I was the only one in the room raising my hand and to help others join me in taking that leap. Improvisation is the perfect tool for this. I decided that people could experience more courage and joy in their lives if they practiced "making stuff up."

PREPARE TO IMPROVISE

WHAT IS IMPROVISATION?

Improvisation (improv) is the art of spontaneous creation, or "just making stuff up." While most think of improvisation as something only jazz musicians or comedians on *Whose Line is it Anyway?* do, we all improvise in some way every day of our lives. We all spend much of our time just making stuff up. Whenever something unexpected happens, we must improvise. We must think and act on the spot. For some of us, this presents interesting opportunities; for others, it feels like a catastrophe.

I started doing improvisation as a way to have more fun as an actor. I found it exhilarating to step onto a bare stage with nothing but my imagination and create something wonderful on the spot. Stage improvisers have nothing planned as we step out there in front of an audience—and we have the time of our lives.

For me, the blank stage represents limitless possibility. But for most people in this world, it is pure terror. Remember when your third-grade teacher asked for someone to come to the front of the room and read aloud from the book? I was that one kid who volunteered so much that eventually my teacher had to preface her request with, "anyone besides Amy." Were you that kid, or were you like 90 percent of the kids who slunk down lower in their desks and avoided eye contact with the teacher at all costs? Did you worry about what would happen if you tripped walking up to the front? Did you imagine coming to a word in the text that you couldn't pronounce? Did you assume this was the day you would let loose the mother of all farts and ruin your reputation before you even had a chance?

Improvisation is being asked to read in front of the class but to leave the book at your desk. So it's just you tripping, making up words, and very likely farting in front of everyone. And then you get lots of applause and people wonder how you can be so brave. This book is about just that and so much more. Stage improvisers are some of the most daring, agreeable, and creative people I have ever met. When we step off stage, the training and preparation we have had does not leave us. It influences *every* aspect of our lives. Improv has made me a happier person. Because of that, I have dedicated my life to sharing this art form with others and using it as a tool for people to take more risks and find more happiness in their lives. When people have the confidence to try new things, meet interesting people, explore a new career, or simply express their thoughts without fear of tripping and farting and ruining their lives, they are happy.

> Improv has made me a happier person. Because of that, I have dedicated my life to sharing this art form with others and using it as a tool for people to take more risks and find more happiness in their lives.

Though I started improvising as a way to show the world how bold and creative and talented I was ("look at me!"), I continued it because of the incredible support and close connections I have made with others who improvise, and because of the hundreds of students from all walks of life who have found that their lives are better if, every now and then, they raise their hand, stand up, laugh more, and, sometimes, just let one rip.

DO YOU WANT TO LIVE MORE LIKE AN IMPROVISER?

Because you are holding this book, chances are you either:

▶ Think improv is fun and want to learn how to apply improv skills to your life. Fantastic! Or,

▶ You think the idea of making things up on stage is absolutely terrifying, and aren't too sure how the strategies used to improvise comedy can help you off stage. Even more fantastic.

Regardless of which camp you fall into, by reading this book you will begin an important journey of growth and self-improvement centered on quieting your inner critic, trusting yourself more, developing more courage, connecting more with others, realizing your full potential, and, most of all—discovering more joy in your life!

These are skills I never expected to learn when I signed up for my first improv class. Yet these are the skills I found most valuable and have since focused all my attention on, on stage and off. And, remember, we are *all* just improvising through life most of the time.

You can easily use the principles I have learned to create the life you've always dreamed of without ever setting foot on stage. As you will discover, learning and practicing improvisation will completely transform your life. Your future will go from a tunnel—just one visible route from point A to point B—to a playground of opportunity in which you have the courage and the tools to choose the game you want to play, and to love doing it! As new things arise in your life, you will know how to embrace the change and add your own contribution to create the best possible outcome.

Throughout this book you are going to meet some of my former and current students, and learn how embracing the lessons of improvisation has changed their lives. Through their stories, you will see how they worked through their anxiety and concerns to:

1) Say "Yes! And . . . "
2) Create more freely
3) Recognize the many gifts in their lives
4) Take more risks
5) Expand their comfort zones
6) Embrace vulnerability and authenticity
7) Harness the power of their ensembles

If you want to open up new possibilities for yourself, improv is for you. If you want to continue doing the same thing every day, being who you or others have pre-determined you are "supposed to" be, and taking shelter in the safety of saying "no," then I will be upfront and tell you this book and this philosophy are not for you. Once you begin practicing the contagious joy of saying, "Yes! And . . . " to yourself, new possibilities will immediately begin to unfold for you. If you are ready to take the first step, then I am so excited to walk this journey with you!

Learning to live like an improviser is a lot like learning to dance; even the best book is no substitute for getting up and just doing it. My hope is that this book prepares and inspires you to take the first step.

Let's play!

SAY "YES! AND . . ."

For more than fifty-five years, improvisers have been studying and practicing the best techniques for crafting action from unlimited possibilities in order to "create something wonderful right away." When we begin a scene we have absolutely no idea what is going to happen. We simply get a suggestion from the audience for inspiration, and we begin acting. And acting, by definition, is doing. We make choices and build on them over and over again. We do this every single show and never run out of new material.

What we have discovered is that the best way to create "something wonderful," scene after scene, night after night, is to respond to absolutely every action or line of dialogue with a "Yes! And . . ." This means we always:

1) Accept whatever idea/choice/action is made by one person
2) Add something to the idea/choice/action that was made

We accept and agree. We agree to the reality that one person has created, and we add to that reality. For example, if I walk on stage and begin a scene by saying "I love your new car!" my partner might respond by saying, "Yes, it's fantastic! I got it for my birthday." My partner has agreed to the reality I have created—that he or she has a new car and it is great—and added something to that creation: that it is a birthday gift.

> Believe it or not, this simple phrase,
> "Yes! And . . ." is the secret of improv.

Believe it or not, this simple phrase, "Yes! And . . ." is the secret of improv. What appears to be super-fast thinking and clever responses on our part is just two ordinary people using the core improv tenet of "Yes! And . . . " If you do this on stage, you can create an engaging, interesting scene. People will probably even laugh with you. If you embrace the "Yes! And . . ." mind-set in your day-to-day communications, you will see monumental changes in your life and in the way people respond to you. If you say "Yes! And . . . " to your *own* ideas, choices, and actions, you will create more wonderful things for yourself in your life!

YES! BUT . . .

When you have an idea, do you celebrate it and act on it? Or do you allow your inner critic to say "Yes! But . . ."? When you think of the career you wish you had or the city you wish you lived in, do you first think, "Yes, but I don't have the right work experience," or "Yes, but it would be so expensive"? We use the words "Yes, but . . ." as a soft "no." And we let that phrase keep us from acting.

True, you might not have the right experience (yet!), and that may be an important factor in how much action you can take.

What action *can* you take right now? "Yes! I am lacking in experience, *and* I can gain experience by asking to assist someone with experience in that position." A simple change in phrasing helps us embrace and add to our ideas instead of stifling them.

You have a successful job in sales, but what you really want is to start your own business. You don't need to say, "Yes! And I will quit this minute and organize an LLC!" Start by agreeing to the reality that you could own your own business without letting the evaluation of the idea stifle your current thoughts. Say "yes" to the reality of owning your own business. Have you truly honored that idea and given it space to exist? Turn the stage lights on it and applaud it. Then let your mind wander a bit with the "Yes! And . . ." mind-set, and ask yourself what you could add to that idea. "Yes, and I would work only from 7 a.m. to 3 p.m." "Yes, and I would sometimes work remotely during the summers in order to take the kids to national parks." "Yes, and I would find a partner with more experience than myself to help me get the business started and to rely on when I need a break." Consider what other skills, strengths, ideas or people you could add to develop this idea further. What might your business be? Who might be involved? What might be great about it? Where might it take you? This is the power of "and."

The point isn't necessarily that you have to start your own business, but rather that you open up new possibilities for yourself and gain practice developing and taking those possibilities further. You may discover when you say "and" to yourself that you don't actually want to start your own business. Maybe what you really want is to do your current job, but to have more freedom and flexibility in your schedule to spend more time with your family. The destination does not need to exactly match your first impulse. In fact, it rarely does. What you are beginning to develop is the improv mind-set. This is the core of how improvisers think. Before jumping to "No," we first say "Yes! And . . ."

The best part about "Yes! And . . ." is that you can start *immediately*. It takes no special equipment or training to begin; it only requires your attention to the opportunities and ideas that arise, and a willingness to explore. The next time someone in your life throws out an idea—be it your boss, your spouse, an employee, a child, or, most importantly, *yourself*—just try agreeing to it and adding to it. Notice how often you say "Yes, but . . ." to yourself or others, and see if you can switch that "but" to an "and" now and then. See where the "and" leads you before you judge the ideas you have. By first saying "Yes! And . . . ," you may discover possibilities that would have lain dormant if you had said, even very reasonably, "yes, but . . . ."

Step out on that stage and see where "Yes! And . . ." might take you. I hope you are as pleasantly surprised as we are each time we do a show.

USING "YES! AND . . ." IN YOUR LIFE

Finest City Improv has helped hundreds of students apply the lessons of improvisation to their lives. By embracing the concept of "Yes! And . . ." and letting go of the "yeah . . . but . . ." mentality that keeps us from realizing new possibilities, our students have accomplished much more than the ability to create a scene on stage.

Bobby Said "Yes! And . . ."

Bobby was someone who always wanted more out of life than his normal 9 to 5, but had little idea how to get there. His normal routine was making him less happy year after year. He finally decided to pursue what he really loved—making people laugh. He started by registering for an improv class.

In improv, Bobby learned to say, "Yes! And . . ." and quickly realized that this was the way he needed to approach every aspect of his life if he was going to begin making changes to become happier. The "Yes! And . . . " mindset was the key to shifting his thinking, and helped him take more risks and pursue his dreams. He kept taking classes, kept getting more opportunities, and, by the end of this year, is planning to be out of the job he hates and making a full-time commitment to the thing he always was "supposed" to be doing: performing. If he hadn't said "Yes! And . . . ," he never would have figured this out and taken steps toward his goal. He has a lot of work to do to reach his objective of becoming a comedian, but he is happier and more energized about life than before he started saying, "Yes! And . . . ."

Bobby has taken the principle improvisers use to create entire worlds on stage to create the life he thought he had missed out on. He said "yes" to his dream of being a performer, something he always felt deep down he was meant to be doing, and said "and" by taking an improv class. And . . . he is taking step after step to get out of the routine that was an obstacle to his happiness.

Bobby is not alone in this kind of transformation. So many students come to Finest City Improv thinking they have missed out on their shot to be great or to have the life they want. Some have put aside their dreams in order to focus on their families. Some feel stuck in a career that matches their expensive degree but does not fulfill them as they imagined. Some feel they simply don't live in the right place or it isn't the right time to pursue what really brings them joy. We all give ourselves many reasons why we haven't or cannot achieve our dreams. Through our classes and our community, they have all found the courage to say "Yes! And . . ." to their current reality *and* to their dreams.

Although I began dancing and acting when I was very young and studied drama in college, my first career was as a video producer. And then I became a librarian! I have a master's degree in library and information science, and though I planned to use it to run a large public library system, I ended up spending about ten years helping biotechnology companies retrieve and manage information. I loved that career for a long time—until, as often happens in life, I found I was missing my first love of acting and considering my next "big thing."

My next thing, as it happened, was opening Finest City Improv. Like so many of you, I was ready for a new challenge and a change from what I had been doing. At the same time, if I had never been a librarian in the corporate world, I am certain I never would have had the capital and the business experience to open my theater as confidently and successfully as I did. My library career provided me with the business acumen and the financial capital to make my dream real.

> When we say, "Yes! And . . . " to ourselves, we never know where it may lead us, but it will often lead us somewhere wonderful.

When we say, "Yes! And . . . " to ourselves, we never know where it may lead us, but it will often lead us somewhere wonderful. It is not too late for you to make your dreams a reality. Everything you have done up to now has provided some preparation for your next big thing, even if it isn't entirely clear how just yet.

Improvisers understand that once something is established on stage it becomes reality. Offstage, we strive to adopt the same philosophy, recognizing and accepting our reality as it is, and moving forward from that space. What resources do you have available to you now? What opportunities are right here on your own stage?

Many of us thwart ourselves in this effort when we say "yes, but . . ." to our own ideas. We accept that we want a new job, but we can't get one because we don't have the right degree, or enough time, or enough money. Focus only on what is real and present in your life right now. Do you have fifteen minutes in the evening to carve out a plan? What experience do you have that will enable you to take on your next big thing, and whom do you know who can help you fill in the gaps? Millions of things in this world do not exist in your life—focus on the things that do exist.

Nowadays, people often ask me, "Do you really do improv full-time?" They are shocked that I am able to live this dream every day, as a career and a life. No side gig required. Though my income has decreased a bit since my librarian days, my happiness has increased immensely. By saying, "Yes! And . . . ," I discovered opportunities I never knew existed and didn't even know I wanted for myself, such as helping hundreds of people find more joy in their own lives every year.

I knew I wanted to be more creative and not give up on my dreams of performing. I had no idea when I said "Yes" to my acting teacher's recommendation to do improvisation that it would bring so much joy to so many people—myself included. The skills of improv prepare you to take advantage of new possibilities to live the life of your dreams by building on what you have right now. I had business skills, and a love of playing and performing. I found, little by little, that improvisation made me a happier person and that I enjoyed helping others discover more joy in their lives with its lessons. No "Yes, but . . ." allowed.

In improv, we must focus on what exists on the stage, refraining from talking too much about people or things that are not present. We keep our attention on the actors performing with us. We concentrate on the relationships being developed and explored in the scene between the characters. We talk to each other about each other and keep the action in the here and now. Off stage, this means keeping our focus on what is present in each moment—particularly, and most importantly, the people in our lives.

Whom do you have in your life that you can put more focus on? I often go into a scene with the intent of finding the other character the most interesting person in the world. Try approaching people in your life whom you know little about in that way. It was the people on my journey from corporate librarian to theater owner who were the most important: the professional speaker, event host, performer, corporate trainer, etc. These were the people who had my back when I didn't know how to get a permit approved by the city or was struggling to mentor new employees.

To this day, it is the relationships I form with people that help me most in achieving my dreams and discovering new possibilities. It is Kat Brown, my very first hire at Finest City Improv, who showed me how much our work was changing people's lives. She finds energy in people's success and well-being, and by becoming interested in her goals and her passions I was able to see the immense value in improvisation beyond the stage.

> Whom in your life can you take a little more interest in and build more authentic and meaningful relationships with?

Whom in your life can you take a little more interest in and build more authentic and meaningful relationships with? When is the last time you sat down with someone you work with outside of work and just got to know each other? Whom can a friend introduce you to who may have experience with what you are looking to achieve? What can you offer them without expecting any assistance in return? This is how we create amazing relationships that tend to lead to "something wonderful" both on- and offstage. The "here and now" leads us to the future we want—if we embrace it and utilize it. Recognize the wealth of possibilities available to you, have the courage to act on just one of them, build on this with "Yes! And . . . ," and create more joy in your life, starting right now!

> Recognize the wealth of possibilities available to you, have the courage to act on just one of them, build on this with "Yes! And . . . ," and create more joy in your life, starting right now!

LET'S PLAY! YES/BUT/NO CONVERSATIONS

The Goal: To experience three distinct ways of conversing on a subject and noticing which leads to the most possibilities

Number of Players: Two

How to Play: Sit face-to-face with a partner. Decide who is Person A and Person B.

Part 1: Person B describes to Person A something he or she enjoyed doing recently. A vacation, an activity, an exciting business venture, anything. Person A actively disengages, stays away from eye contact and interjects non-sequiturs. Person B tries to continue to tell his or her story for at least two minutes.

Part 2: Person A talks about something he or she wants to do in the near future. It could be work-related, a vacation, lunch, or whatever. Person B continously replies with "Yes, but . . ." Person B's job is to constantly tell Person A why it's a bad idea. Person A tries to maintain his or her enthusiasm for the future endeavor.

Part 3: Person B offers an idea of something he or she should do with Person A, such as surfing, dinner at a nice restaurant, a trip to Hawaii, etc. Person A responds with "Yes, and we . . . ." Then person B responds with "Yes, and . . . ." And so on back and forth, always responding with "Yes! And . . ." to each other's ideas and then adding something new.

Why We Play It: Extremes show us that "Yes, and . . ." leads to the most action, enjoyment and possibilities. Although we don't always say no, we say "yes, but . . ." much more often in our lives than we realize. Notice this in your life!

PLEASE PUT ON YOUR OWN OXYGEN MASK FIRST

If you have been on an airplane, you have heard the flight attendants tell you that, in the event of an emergency, you are to put on your own oxygen mask before assisting others. They say this because if you aren't able to breathe, you aren't going to be able to help anyone else.

In improv, we call this taking care of yourself first. Agreeing and adding to what is said is the most important thing in improv, but we can't start that process unless someone in the scene makes an initial choice to say or do something. Have you ever tried to make dinner plans with someone, and both of you insist you don't care where you go? This kind of stalemate is exactly what happens when improvisers attempt to support each other without taking care of themselves first.

Improvisers entering a scene are taught to be ready to act first by making a clear choice about who they are that can carry them through the scene. It can be something as simple as "I'm happy" or choosing to carry themselves in a certain way. I've seen hundreds of scenes start with two people staring at each other, each person waiting for the other to make the first choice in order to be "the supportive one." You are being just as supportive if you make an offer. I've also seen hundreds of scenes by beginning improvisers where one makes an offer and the other is visibly relieved. We just need something to start with.

It is certainly true that great things come about when you keep an open mind and stand ready to say "Yes!" to the opportunities that come your way. But it is much more fruitful for everyone if you take opportunities to initiate ideas and actions as often as you stand ready to offer support for them. The next excercise in this chapter will help you find small ways to create action even when you feel like all the oxygen is escaping, and the proverbial plane is nose-diving to a fiery crash because no one is taking action or making a choice.

LET'S PLAY! LEAD WITH ANYTHING

The Goal: To discover new points of view, using physical movements to inspire us

Number of Players: Any

How to Play: Stand up and walk around whatever room you are in at a normal pace and in whatever way feels normal and natural for you. After about 30 seconds, pick a body part. Whatever body part comes to mind first is the correct one. Now, adjust your walk so you are leading with that body part. If you chose your nose, lead with your nose. If you chose your right knee, lead with your right knee. There is no right way to lead with your nose or right knee, so don't worry about doing this perfectly; just do it in whatever way you feel compelled to. Imagine there is a pane of glass in front of you, and your goal is to have the leading body part break that glass.

Next, exaggerate this walk. Change anything else about your motion that you feel goes with the walk you have discovered you are doing. Maybe you started by leading with your shoulders and hunching them over, and this compels you to slow down. You then notice you feel like putting a scowl on your face. This inspires you to shuffle your feet.

Now, allow yourself to make a sound that a person who walks like this might make. Does this person laugh? Cough? Sigh? Grumble? Try it out!

Finally, name the person you have become. Give yourself the first name that comes to your mind.

Why We Play It: This exercise is a fantastic illustration of what can come about when you say "yes, and . . ." At first, all I asked you to do was pick a body part. Did you have any idea whom you were going to become in that moment? Did you guess that by leading with your shoulders you would become Grumpy Grandma Guthrie? Or Ronnie the rough and tumble rugby player? Of course not! You simply started with one small action, said "yes" to it, *and* added the next thing that built on that first thing. When you use the tool of "Yes! And . . . ," you remain in the present moment and build on what was just offered to you either by yourself or someone else. Take one little step (in this case, sometimes literally), and then discover what feels right with that movement. We play this over and over again to see all the different characters we have inside of us. This is the same way many of the characters you see and love on TV sketch comedy shows were discovered.

THREE WAYS TO ADD THE "AND . . ."

TRUST YOUR INSTINCTS

One of the most difficult things about learning to improvise is accepting that whatever you say or do is the right choice in that moment. I know what you're thinking: how can everything be the right choice? In improv, our goal is to create something. As long as you are agreeing to the reality ("yes") and adding something of yourself to it ("and"), you will create something new in that moment. There is no wrong way to do it.

I once performed in a scene where I was a middle-school girl who was stuffing her bra. When prompted to reveal what she was stuffing it with, I blurted out the very first thing that came to mind: "tuna fish." I immediately thought that was just about the dumbest thing I could have possibly said in that moment. After all, who stuffs their bra with tuna fish? However, using the tool of "Yes! And . . . ," my teammates turned it into a fantastic scene. To this day, I have members of that audience coming up to me, saying, "Remember the tuna fish scene? That was hilarious!"

Now, don't get too scared: I don't expect you to tell strangers you are stuffing your bra with tuna fish. The point is that improv gives you practice in speaking your mind, trusting your gut and saying whatever is true for you in the moment—even if it is scary and even if you don't totally understand it yet. Because improvisers have practiced trusting and acting on their instincts in classes, they have the muscle memory to do it in real life.

For example, if improvisers see someone they are attracted to, they have the confidence and skills to say so, even knowing that others might consider them weird and that it might not go the way they would like. We have no idea what the outcome will be when we follow our instincts. Maybe we will find true love, maybe we'll meet a cute friend, or maybe we will just get a great story. But we do know the outcome of saying "no" to ourselves: we stay sitting on that barstool, stirring the ice in our drink, and wishing our life was different. I know which option I would choose, and I think you know which one you would prefer, too.

LET'S PLAY! ELECTRIC COMPANY

The Goal: To keep a consistent rhythm as you create two-word combinations

Number of Players: Two or more

How to Play: Two people can play this face-to-face, or you can add people by standing in a circle. Start with everyone snapping their fingers to establish a slow beat. You can get faster as you learn the basics. On one snap, one person says a single-syllable word—any word! The point is to say the first word that comes to mind. The person next to them says another word on the next snap. This person says the first word that comes to mind based on the word the first person says. The goal is to have no hesitation so that you keep the rhythm. Once both words are spoken, everyone repeats them together. For example: Person A says "green," Person B says "flash," then everyone says "green flash." For fun, you can add "da-do-da-do" after that. On the very next snap, Person B says a brand-new word and Person C (or A if just two of you) says the next word. Again, everyone repeats. Continue around the circle (or back and forth for a pair) many times and see how fast you can go.

Why We Play It: Everyone has a critical side that evaluates what we say, often before we say it. This serves us well in many situations, but can also work against us if it causes us to freeze up. Have fun "failing" at this game. Let a silly noise out if that is what comes out! This is your chance to practice removing the filter and being OK if the "perfect answer" doesn't materialize. Just work to stay on the beat and notice how fun it is when everyone supports you and says both words together with excitement!

HEIGHTEN EVERYTHING

One way we can say "and" to our own ideas is by heightening them. In improv lingo, this means taking them a step further. Escalating the stakes. If I start a scene by saying, "I'm smart," I might heighten it by adding, "I have a Ph.D." I could heighten it further by saying that I've published over one thousand articles. And that I invented space travel!

By heightening our ideas to the extreme on the stage, we often take them to outrageous places. It sometimes takes us out of the realm of realism—of course I did not invent space travel—but it keeps things interesting and helps us explore the outer reaches of our ideas. By considering "what is the biggest this can be?" we are able to fully flesh out and explore an idea that, on its surface, might not be very interesting at all.

In the day-to-day, this might mean saying your goal is to exercise for 30 minutes, four days a week. That's a pretty nice goal all on its own, but just as a thought workout, let's heighten it. What if you added that it was going to be 30 minutes of bike riding? Down a mountain. In South America. With your child strapped to your back.

Whoa, Nelly! Now that's a heck of an interesting scenario. Does this mean it's ultimately a good idea? Not at all. But by exploring ways to heighten your idea, you've generated fresh, new ideas. Taken all together, that workout regime is probably a little intense for most of us, but it might make you realize that you'd like to take your workout outside or involve your family.

By freeing your mind from the constraint of the ordinary, you open yourself up to new opportunities for joy and growth.

IF THIS IS TRUE, WHAT ELSE IS TRUE?

I also teach beginning improv students to take what exists in a scene and ask, "If this is true, what else is true?" This line of thinking is an especially good way to develop a character. For example, it has been established that a character named Jenny likes birds. Well, if this is true, what else is true? Maybe Jenny has a parrot, and that parrot is her very best friend in the world. Maybe Jenny spends her spare time trying to build human-scale wings so she can fly like her feathered friends!

In improv, we are making it all up on the spot, so whatever we say about Jenny automatically becomes true for that scene. It is interesting to know that Jenny likes birds, but it is a lot more interesting and a lot richer to know that she likes them so much she is compelled to invent a new flying apparatus.

The same goes for you. Take something you like about yourself or that you love doing and pretend for a moment that you are imagining someone else. If this is true about them, what else might they be good at? What else might they love pursuing? Who else would be a great connection for them? What other connections should they be making? Whom should they be meeting to make those connections?

You are more than any one piece of yourself: more than your job, your degree, or even your passion. You are brimming with possibility and untapped courage. Take this opportunity to explore yourself like an improviser. I hope you are surprised and delighted by what you discover.

> By freeing your mind from the constraint of the ordinary, you open yourself up to new opportunities for joy and growth.

CHAPTER SUMMARY

▶ "Yes! And . . ." means agree to the idea and contribute something.

▶ Saying "Yes! And . . ." creates the greatest amount of action.

▶ "Yes, but . . ." is just like "No." Become more aware of its use.

▶ Your first choice is an acceptable choice. Roll with it!

▶ Heighten and explore your choices to see where they lead.

CREATE NOW. EVALUATE LATER

At some point in our life, usually when we are children, we are criticized in a way that cuts to our core. The message received is that we are not good enough. For me, it happened when I was 15 years old. I was a great actor but was not cast as the lead in *Grease* at school because I didn't sing well. I had a Frenchie voice, not a Sandra voice. Well, that's how I interpreted the casting and hence told myself, "I can't sing." And so I didn't. Not for a long, long time. In reality, I was just more of a character actor and best-suited for the part of funny and quirky Frenchie.

That critical voice moves into your mind on that day, takes up residence and continues to whisper in your ear. It tells you that your ideas are no good, that you shouldn't even bother trying and that you are not good enough. When we become adults, we have been listening to this voice for so long we assume what it tells us is true. After all, it is in our own head; why would it lie?

It would be naïve of me to suggest you should get rid of that voice. For most of us, it has been around so long it would be impossible to do so. It serves us well in many situations. However, many people pay too much attention to that voice. It's fine to let it say its piece, to acknowledge and accept that it is there without accepting that it is right. From there, tune into what the rest of you is saying.

Do you feel joy when you sing? That is just as important as what the little voice says. Do you feel calm when you sing? That is just as important. Are you ignited and creative? That is just as important. The more you tune in to *all* of yourself, the more those objective, real and joyful voices will begin to outweigh the single, critical, 15-year-old voice. And, really, who cares if you sound like a bad pop singer without auto tune as long as it makes you feel wonderful?! Now I happily sing with a musical improv group in front of many—and though I still don't have the voice of Olivia Newton-John, I have a lot of fun with it!

This is crucial because that judgmental voice is pure evaluation. It will never create anything. It only halts creation. As improvisers, we seek to create first and evaluate later. Doing so lifts the feeling of obligation that everything we create be good, because we are not yet evaluating whether something is good at all. It doesn't matter; all that matters is that you are creating something.

Why do this if, ultimately, your goal is to create something good? First, we do this because it frees us to create quantity, unburdened by quality. With this shift in focus, we arrive at fifty potential ideas instead of five evaluated ideas. If we take the time to evaluate every creative impulse, and the best idea is number 47, we will never even get there. There just isn't enough time. Secondly, ideas build on each other. Idea number six is the inspiration for idea number seven, and so on. They are inextricable.

Jesse Created a Life He Loved

Several years ago Jesse was living on the East Coast, and he felt like he had his life really together. He was performing stand-up comedy regionally, was outgoing and fun at parties, and had a ton of friends and a wonderful relationship.

At the end of 2012, the boyfriend he describes as the love of his life passed away, followed by one of his best friends a week later in a car crash. After just one more week, his sister died. Jesse's life crashed down around him, and he was a wreck. He tried everything from therapy to simply locking himself away from the world. All to no avail.

He moved to San Diego to get a fresh start and to get away from the memories. When he arrived, he struggled with social anxiety and had a lot of trouble making new friends and letting down his walls. He wandered by our doors one day and picked up our flier. It took him awhile to get started, but as he got to know us a bit more, he decided to give it a try. When he first started taking classes at Finest City Improv, he says, he was terrified. However, a few months into his improv training, he told us he feels not only like his old self again, but also like an even better version of himself!

He told me he talks to people again, like he used to. Even after facing overwhelming tragedy, he feels like he has permission to be funny. He has made many great friendships. But the truth is that once Jesse let down his walls, he became a magnet for joyful interaction. He is the kind of person everyone wants to be around. His smile and joy are simply infectious.

Jesse has applied the principles of improv to his life, tapping into his core and unleashing his true nature. In his own words, Jesse says, "Improv has been the best therapy/life coach/pill a person like me could have asked for."

The most important lesson Jesse learned from practicing improv is to take care of himself first. He is naturally a warm, giving person, but in order to keep that alive, he had to learn how to create joy for himself first. In order to spread infectious happiness, he had to create a life he loved for himself. Once he did, he began creating happiness for others, which is his true calling.

When he signed up for his first improv class, he had no intentions other than to get out of his rut and meet people. Now he is feeling the same way I do about improvisation and the joy that teaching it brings to others. Last fall he decided he wanted more improv in his life. He told me, "I'm going to work for you." I had no job openings, but I agreed to have dinner with him to get to know him better and hear about his goals. Little by little he found ways to be of help around the theater, beginning by volunteering to run lights and sound.

Eventually, his "Yes! And . . ." attitude created opportunities for him. He is now a part-time employee managing many of our business operations, supervising technical operations, and even teaching our introductory improv courses. Best of all, his amazing attitude toward jumping in with both feet has made him the self-proclaimed "pageant mom" for me whenever I have an important event. I can't imagine life at Finest City Improv without Jesse, and I am so glad we said, "Yes! And . . ." to each other.

Improvisers get up on an empty stage with nothing but each other. We have no script, no scenery, no props—not even imaginary ones at that point. We begin by requesting a one-word suggestion or phrase from the audience as inspiration. From there, we connect with each other by making eye contact—and right there, in that moment, we have absolutely everything we need. More so, even, than a scripted performer would have because we can conjure any costumes or props we can imagine. The possibilities are limitless. We just need to take action. Any action.

We don't wait until we have a good idea, or we think our scene partner does. We certainly don't wait until the laundry is done, the kids are grown, or we've lost those last five pounds. We just start right where we are, with the first thought or action that presents itself. We make a physical, emotional, or verbal contribution to get the scene started, and we are on our way.

The most successful people do exactly the same thing in their lives and businesses. If they had waited until someone provided the capital they needed, until they knew everything they could about how to proceed, or—least likely—until life finally calmed down, they never would have begun. Great things are not accomplished on stage or in business because of a single brilliant idea or person, but because someone had the courage to begin and the tenacity to continue. Successful people don't wait for the speaker to toss them the tennis ball; they raise their hand and volunteer!

> Start where you are. Immediately.
> The longer you wait to make that
> move, the more pressure you put on
> yourself to get it perfectly right.

Start where you are. Immediately. The longer you wait to make that move, the more pressure you put on yourself to get it perfectly right. The longer you think about that move, the more you expect it to be fantastic. What if you just took a step and got the scene started?

As children, most of us played games with few rules. You probably remember playing dozens of variations of tag. You and your friends would decide to play, start running, and something surprising or delightful would happen (bumping into another player, for example), and you turned that into a new rule of the game.

Just start the game. Discover what's possible as you play. That's how we get started on an empty stage with hundreds of expectant audience members. Get your inspiration and make that first simple move *now*.

LET'S PLAY! SEVEN THINGS

The Goal: To list seven things in rapid succession without hesitating

Number of Players: One to sixteen

How to Play: One player calls out a category, such as "Seven things you'd find in a car!" That person then points to another player to begin listing seven things in that category as fast as possible. The entire group cheers the player on by enthusiastically counting after each item is named. If you are playing alone, you can challenge yourself to categories.

Why We Play It: At first this game seems simple. We are given a word like "car," and we can immediately name something obvious like "seats" or "steering wheel." So, first we practice naming something immediately—but we're just getting started! Once you are good at getting those first few words out, practice keeping the rhythm and not hesitating as you continue to list things. After about four words most people start to hesitate. At this point, just continue to list things—anything! If you say "rhino," that is better than silence or "umm." The idea is to give yourself permission to say whatever comes to mind first! Besides, the idea of a rhino riding in a car is kind of fun.

BRING A BRICK, NOT A CATHEDRAL

You'll hear improv teachers say this a lot, especially to newer improvisers. What we mean is that you do not need to bring a fully formed idea into a scene. Instead, simply bring one small piece of information or one simple action. You do not need the blueprint to begin laying bricks. The cathedral represents a sacred goal you have to aim for, and at best it will get a few mediocre laughs. Instead, we prefer to contribute a simple idea and see where it leads us. No blueprint. No worries.

I completely understand that "leaping without looking" is a terrifying prospect, and you probably feel like this is beyond your current abilities. I work with hundreds of students both at our training center and at companies, and this is the skill we work most on. We all have a little inner critic and a spectacularly trained logical and analytical adult brain that have kept us safe and helped us make great decisions in our life. But they have also held us back at times by keeping us within a defined comfort zone. I long believed I couldn't sing. I always lamented the fact that I could dance and act well but could not sing. This held me back from auditioning for musicals, and I missed out on being in many shows I absolutely love.

A few years ago, I really wanted to be able to do musical improvisation and have a musical improv group play on our stage. Having a few years of improvisation under my belt and now living the principles it had taught me, I said, "why not?!" I formed a group and filled it with fun improvisers. Some were great singers and others, like me, had very little practice singing. Notice I don't say ability to sing. What I've learned from improv is to allow my brain to assume that everyone has the ability. That provided me with the possibility that I could practice and get better at it. Previously, I would tell myself, "I don't have a singing voice." Honestly, that was a safer route to take then trying to sing and having my ego crushed when people winced or laughed at me. Many years later, the group is still going strong—and I'm still not the best singer. But I have an incredible amount of fun doing musical improvisation. I still feel anxious about my singing voice, but I am having fun being the one who sings "like a rock 'n' roll ballad singer."

I get it. Creating without evaluating is a scary, vulnerable move. It leaves you open to failing spectacularly and having your ego crushed. The alternative, though, is inaction. When I teach improv, I never concern myself with the result of whatever action students take. As we say so often in improv, "There is no wrong answer or choice"—as long as you make one. So we repeatedly play games that help you take that first step without concern for what comes next. You would not do this for an important life decision or something where you truly risk harm. But in an improv class, where everyone is committed to "just go for it," and every move results in thunderous applause, we start to build the ability to take action. We start to develop more comfort in creating without first evaluating.

Ask yourself, when was the last time you did something without first analyzing the likelihood of success or failure? When you go to a new restaurant, do you send the server away multiple times so you can spend more time deciding on the "right" dinner for that moment? Or do you ask what is good and go with that without even looking at the menu? Perhaps you are somewhere in between. What improv helps you do is sit down and ask the server to surprise and delight you with a delicious appetizer to share with the table.

Like sitting down to an unplanned dinner at an unfamiliar restaurant, the best improv scenes often start out simply and without any pre-evaluation of possible outcomes. They begin with a simple offer rather than a premise and, bit-by-bit, they build, gathering momentum as the pieces come together with the help of the collective. I'll order a mai tai; you will find my choice delightful, order the same and ask for cute little umbrellas on them. The server will recommend the pupu platter with the mai tais, and we will agree. The ideas discovered through this process are surprisingly delightful and usually funnier than anything we could have planned. I created that example as I typed, without planning the metaphor. I imagined sitting in a restaurant and typed the first type of drink that came to my head. I did not judge it before I typed it, and did not go back and change it. Now that I can evaluate it, I find it quite fun!

This distinction can be hard to spot, and audiences often assume our approach is to practice thinking of amazing ideas as fast as possible until we become the wittiest people in the room. Or that we create situations and direct them for each other from within the acting. Audiences often assume improvisers are writing a story on the stage, knowing from the beginning how the characters connect and what the moral or punch line will be. We don't do either of those things. In fact, those are two great ways to ensure a bad show full of . . . well, bullshit. No matter how hard we might try to direct the action, without a script it will never happen as we expect. And that, too, is life.

The truth is that we just allow ourselves to create without evaluating. We are saying to our inner critic, "Save your energy for analyzing mortgage rates tomorrow; I've got this right now." We take a suggestion and allow it to inspire us to create something simple with the first choice or action we think of. Sometimes it's simply bouncing up and down. Sometimes it's a proclamation of love for the other character. Sometime we just begin typing on a computer. We each offer one little piece and build with them together, having no idea at all what we are building, focusing only on the moment at hand and having fun with each other.

I begin jumping for joy. Brick.

You smile and wish me good morning. Brick.

I say I am excited for morning because it's pancake day. Brick.

You tell me you're putting bananas and walnuts in the pancakes today. Brick.

I tell you "I love you, Mom!" Brick.

Each piece builds on the last. Going somewhere amazing does not mean knowing where you are going. The path only reveals itself at the destination. Brick by brick the castle reveals itself to us. In the end, we sometimes have a decrepit old haunted house, and other times we have that bouncy castle our parents never let us have at our birthday party. Whatever it is, we don't find out and evaluate until it's over. Even then, we usually just focus on what was awesome and fun about it. That's a pretty cool way to approach life.

Have you ever wondered what it would be like to go to the airport, passport in hand, and book the first flight to wherever it is going? That would be a huge step. With improv we can get that feeling through playing games, building the courage to create now and evaluate later.

We can do this in life by sharing our own ideas before they are fully formed or taking a different route home from work. We can do it when thinking about our ideas and goals in life. Give your ideas space to grow before you evaluate and stifle them. You can give them permission to be just a brick within a larger structure. Or you can say "no" or "yes, but . . ." to them.

So many people never begin because they don't think their ideas are good enough. But the only way they can become great ideas is if you give them space to exist in the first place. Try the "Seven Things" game I described by yourself or with friends. Then try using this process once a day when you have an idea for the future or are presented with an unexpected possibility. In fact, write them down instead of just saying them. And do *not* evaluate any of them until they are all written out. Let your ideas out to play.

> Let your ideas out to play.

Remember, you have a ton of ideas, more than you are fully aware of. The goal is to treat them each as just one little brick in a magical castle being built without a blueprint. You can supply some of the bricks, but the world must supply some as well. So you will have to learn to pay attention like an improviser, noticing every little thing you see, hear and sense. What are others saying? How are they standing? What conversations are happening in your community? Where is the wind blowing today? Improvisers pay rapt attention to the details, because that is where the inspiration lies.

LET'S PLAY! WORD-AT-A-TIME STORIES

The Goal: To tell a story that makes sense but with each person adding just one word at a time

Number of Players: Two or more

How to Play: With a friend (or two or three), sit in a circle and tell a story one word at a time. Going in order from person to person, each one of you offers the next word in the story. Rather than try to steer the story in your own direction, or even toward anything particularly logical, pay close attention to what the person right before you said, and simply add the next word that fits. Continue until the story comes to a natural end.

Why We Play It: Letting go of control and creating something one piece at a time can be scary the first time you try it. This exercise is a safe way to practice contributing your piece, while also accepting and building with—not against—the reality around you over which you have no control. Practice like this creates the muscle memory you need to keep this same mind-set of acceptance and action as you create your life. Try this exercise to work this muscle and get it ready to do some heavy lifting in your life.

YOU DON'T HAVE TO START AT THE BEGINNING

Exposition can be boring. In storytelling, we understand that it's necessary. In stories, exposition establishes where the story takes place and who the characters are. But it's the juicy action, the declaration of love or the moment of truth that keeps us sitting on the edge of our seat. Amid all your excitement about your next big thing, I bet there is a piece you are dreading that keeps you from moving forward. I'll bet anything it's the exposition. Just getting started is the hardest part.

The lesson from improv is to skip it. For now, that is. That's right, just skip right past the daunting unknown of the exposition and jump right into the delicious action. Jesse let himself jump into an improv class with no plan for how it would inform his career choices. It turns out that was the beginning of a new life for him. He thought it would just be a fun hobby leading toward other goals.

Improvisers do this all the time. We start scenes right after the girl has confessed her love—we can get to where she is and how they met later. This is the exciting part for the actors and the audience! What is the exciting part of your dream? All dreams worth pursuing have scary "getting started" details, but they also have a joyful, beautiful middle.

What is one piece of your next big
thing you can start right now?

What is one piece of your next big thing you can start right now? Think for a moment and identify one thing you can do in the next fifteen minutes that is the meaty, juicy, exciting part of your next big thing. If you want to open an artisanal Parisian bakery, bake a loaf of bread. If you want to sell your art, paint. If you want to write a book, write. Skip over the planning, the financing and the making time. You can get there later.

Can I let you in on a secret? I didn't start this book at the beginning. I didn't even start by making an outline. I started right here, by sitting down and writing this very chapter. Of course, eventually I made an outline and wrote the beginning and the end, but at the time the most important thing was simply to start. For two hours every morning I wrote the thoughts I had about how improv has improved my life and the lives of others.

Starting in the middle, with the piece you are most excited about, connects you with the heart of your work and the joy of where you are headed. Without this connection and joy, the fear of the unknown that lives in the beginning of a change can be so daunting it will deter you from ever beginning.

LET'S PLAY! AMAZING MACHINE

The Goal: To create an amazing machine as a group, each contributing one piece of the machine

Number of Players: Best with five to twelve players.
How to Play: Stand in a circle. One person steps forward into the circle and begins a repetitive motion and sound. Immediately following this initiation, another player adds

the next piece of the machine with a different sound and motion, connecting to the first player. Continue until all players are a part of the machine except one. The remaining player immediately calls out a name for this amazing machine. Repeat this process a few times, creating many amazing machines.

Why We Play It: We learn a lot about ourselves when we notice whether we are hesitant to initiate the machine or to add to the machine. We all have a critic inside of us that would like to have the whole machine perfectly worked out before we know how we fit in it. This game helps us practice jumping in and building the machine without knowing what kind of machine we are making. We just start building and end up delighted by the results.

CHAPTER SUMMARY:

▶ Take the first step without worrying if it's "right."
▶ You do not need to know what you are building to create something great; just bring a single brick.
▶ Focus on what exists in the present moment, rather than on what is wrong or how you wish things had been.
▶ The beginning is hard to envision. You can start in the middle.

GIVE AND RECEIVE GIFTS

A t some point in your life, your parents probably gave up trying to surprise you with a great birthday gift. Now they just give you a gift card or some cash and say, "Get yourself something you actually want." My mother asks me about a month before my birthday to send her some ideas of something she can get me. I usually wrack my brain to think of something that will be meaningful and that I would not normally get for myself, like a necklace or a day at a spa. Every now and then she will surprise me with something I never asked for or have not seen before—although sometimes it's a bar of goat milk soap from her beloved Beekman Boys, which leaves my hands smelling like I just petted a goat. Still, I always cherish these fun little surprises.

When we say, "Yes! And . . ." we have two important responsibilities. First, we have to accept that what has been offered is a gift—a delightful gift. Second, we have to give gifts ourselves.

When we get gifts, especially from our parents, they are sometimes not what we expected. Usually, they are not the expensive sailing jacket and pants we wished for. Nevertheless, it is our responsibility to appreciate these gifts for what they are. As you know, if we ever want to get another gift, we have to be excited about and thankful for the gifts people give us. Why would it be any different when people offer their ideas, dreams, and goals? Why would you treat *yourself* and your ideas, dreams, and goals any differently?

We also have to give gifts. If I show up to enough parties without a bottle of wine for the host, I should expect they would do the same when I host a party. Heck, I shouldn't expect to get invited back. Similarly, if I don't share my ideas, dreams, and goals with others, why would they be interested in sharing theirs with me? Treat these like gifts. I'll offer mine, and I hope you will then want to offer yours.

My goal is to get one million people to read this book and every one of them to watch an improv show or take an improv class. My dream is to spend a large portion of my life writing more books and teaching about improv while living on a sailboat in the Virgin Islands. Now that you know, I hope you will share this book with a friend. That would be an incredible gift. What are your ideas, dreams, and goals? When is the last time you asked someone close to you about theirs?

> What are your ideas, dreams, and goals? When is the last time you asked someone close to you about theirs?

As improvisers, we learn to treat everything that's said and done on stage as a gift, something the players can take and use to make the scene more interesting. We don't know what to expect, but we have the intention to love it and find something wonderful about it. If we all have this intention, we eventually create a show full of wonderful, positive, interesting, and engaging moments. By saying "Yes!" we are accepting the gift (or offer for the scene) as exactly what we wanted, and by adding "And . . . ," we are saying thank you and, in a way, adding why it is the perfect gift! "Yes! We are in love. And . . . we are eloping today!" "Yes! I am your barber. And . . . my haircuts give you confidence."

LET'S PLAY! THE GIFT-GIVING GAME

The Goal: To name gifts for ourselves that spark a feeling of joy and possibilities

Number of Players: Two (or more, in pairs)

How to Play: Stand facing your partner. Decide on Person A and Person B. Person A turns and pretends to pick up something behind her. She does not need to pretend it has shape or size or weight. At this point no one knows what it is. Person A hands the imaginary gift to Person B and says, with great excitement, "I got you a gift!" Person B takes the imaginary gift and replies, "Thank you for the _____." Person B finishes the sentence with the first thing that comes to mind. He should not wait to reply. He should start the "Thank you" immediately and with gusto, and see how the sentence almost finishes itself. Once Person B names the gift, Person A responds, "You're welcome!" and the gift disappears. Repeat this with each person taking turns being the gift giver and the receiver. Remember, the person receiving the gift names it. Repeat at least 10 times without a break. Then discuss the gifts that were received.

Why We Play It: When students first play this game, they tend to think hard about what they will name each gift. As the game progresses and they begin naming gifts with a feeling of abandon, the gifts become more interesting, more fun, and less serious. They also become more positive and more imaginative. Practice giving yourself wonderful gifts!

Notice that I insist that we give with enthusiasm, receive with a heartfelt "Thank you!" and conclude each transaction with "You're welcome!" I do this so that we practice making every transaction with others an important and meaningful moment in our lives. Don't miss a single chance to let others know how grateful you are for any bit of support, encouragement, or gift of any type they take the time to offer.

Fill in the blank with whatever first comes to mind. Simple, right? Your gift could be a shiny red convertible, a puppy, a million dollars, a hot dog—anything you decide! The gift can be anything the receiver decides he or she wants it to be.

After a few rounds I ask participants what they received. Many people recount receiving wonderful gifts. One client even said she received a perfect gift: the gift of more time! But several people will scoff and say, "I got dirty dishes!" or "I got smelly socks!" What a terrible gift!

"Who gave you that gift?" I ask them. In improv a lot of things are totally unpredictable, but with nearly 100 percent certainty, I can tell you how this person will reply: "My partner gave it to me."

Sorry, but your partner did not give you that gift. Your partner simply held out his or her hands and offered up a blank slate of possibility. If you got smelly socks as a gift, it is because you decided on it.

"Oh, I guess I did," they say, as I watch the gears click into place in their mind.

We make these decisions offstage every day when we decide what gifts we want to receive from the world and how we want to give the gift of ourselves to the world. Of course, not everything feels like a gift. The tax return I am avoiding picking up from my tax preparer is going to include a bill that certainly won't feel like a gift. Taxes and death are inevitable, and I don't think either of those is a gift. I have no positive spin to put on either one.

However, we experience thousands of moments and many interactions with others in which it is up to us to decide what role they play in our life. A gift could be the few minutes of extra sleep you allowed yourself this morning or the few minutes earlier that you got up. It could be the few minutes extra you allow yourself to sit on the front porch, coffee in hand, enjoying the morning sunshine. These are little gifts we can notice, say "Yes!" to, *and* add our appreciation *and* give our full presence to. Everything around you impacts your life, but it is up to you what you bring in and accept as a gift.

I share a fantastic fable known as the "Taoist Farmer" with my advanced students (thanks to Pam Victor for first sharing it with me). This story is sometimes referred to as the "Maybe" story. In this story, an old farmer's horse runs away. His neighbors come to visit and say, "Such bad luck," sympathetically. The farmer simply replies, "Maybe." The next morning the horse returns, bringing with it three other wild horses. "How wonderful," the neighbors exclaim. "Maybe," replies the old man. The following day, his son tries to ride one of these untamed horses, is thrown, and breaks his leg. The neighbors again come to offer their sympathy on his misfortune. "Maybe," the farmer replies. The day after, military officials come to the village to draft young men into the army. Seeing that the son's leg is broken, they pass him by. The neighbors congratulate the farmer on how well things turned out. "Maybe," says the farmer.

The wise farmer does not let judgment of each event in the story turn into a cause for anxiety, anger, or sadness. Instead, he keeps an open mind and imagines that each might just as well lead to a positive outcome. He accepts the reality and incorporates it into his life, just as we teach improvisers to accept the reality established as a gift and add something to it.

I encourage you to find more moments like this in your interactions with others in life. If you walk up to that attractive man or woman and introduce yourself, might that individual make you feel stupid for doing so? Maybe. Might he or she have been working up the courage to come talk to you and be grateful you made the first move? Maybe. If neither of you makes a move, will anything happen? Maybe, but it's a lot less likely. I believe—and improv helps me take this risk—that if I introduce myself to that person I am giving him or her a gift.

The individual may not expect it or be delighted by it, but in general everyone enjoys receiving a gift. What is the gift? It's myself, my attention, my interest in that person, my willingness to take the first step. I know it feels great when others give me those things, so I also must be willing to give.

Improvisers are masters of paying attention to everything happening around us. We call the little things we notice "gifts" because every little piece can be used to benefit our performance.

> As we go through our daily lives,
> we can choose to put our blinders on
> and complain, or to consider everything
> happening around us as a gift.

As we go through our daily lives, we can choose to put our blinders on and complain, or to consider everything happening around us as a gift. You never know if the person behind you in line at the coffee shop is your next business partner, client or mentor. Great ideas don't pop up out of nowhere—although it often feels like they do. They are the product of our brains forming lots and lots of new synapses and connections and, eventually, connecting all the pieces. In order for this process to happen, you have to gather a lot of pieces.

I encourage you to adopt the improviser's mind-set that each moment is a gift. Pay close attention to the people you interact with and to the simple, tactile experience of living, whether it is a barista who could use your sympathetic ear or a quiet moment for self-reflection in the midst of a chaotic day. Each moment holds a gift if we are looking for it. What opportunities might you catch if you approached each day in this way?

Likewise, you get to define for yourself how you want to give the gift of yourself to the world. Make no mistake; you are absolutely a gift to the world. Sometimes, though, we fail to recognize that or feel that way. I invite you to dig deep and declare your gift. Are you a rockin' musician? Name it! Are you a brilliant engineer? Say it! Are you a great friend? Label it! Give your gift a fantastic name. Give it a name you can fall in love with and get excited about. Now treat that gift with respect and care, even if not everyone around you understands it. That's OK; not everyone has to.

Some days my gift is "maestro." Some days it is "supporter." It can change with your moods because you have many different things to offer many different people. What are yours?

BUT I REALLY DO GET CRAPPY GIFTS!

I understand that the dishes are real, the laundry is real, the grocery shopping is real, and the unread pile of e-mails is real. However, just because they really do exist does not mean they have to be a roadblock to living more fully and more joyfully now. The incomplete task list is the ultimate "Yes, but . . ." monster. By saying "Yes, but . . . ," you acknowledge your dreams and your potential and, in one fell swoop, you shoot them down. "Yes, but . . ." closes down possibilities. Give yourself permission to imagine life outside of that nagging "must-do" list. You really do have a choice. Choosing a different gift does not mean failing to acknowledge reality. It means accepting your role as the master of your own story.

Practice in little ways now so when it comes time to decide if you will follow your dreams, you will be ready to recognize and say "Yes, and . . ." to them.

CHAPTER SUMMARY:

▶ You deserve to create gifts for yourself as much as you deserve to receive great gifts.
▶ You define the gifts you bring to the world.
▶ Open yourself up to "Yes! And . . . ." That is, all the gifts, good and "bad," that you are presented with.
▶ Stay present and be ready to receive unexpected gifts.

FAIL SPECTACULARLY
AND REPEATEDLY

Three of the most common human fears are public speaking, failure, and spiders. While improvisers have no special immunity against spiders, practicing improv is the ultimate exposure therapy for the first two. And by the way, you are much, much bigger than a spider, and the vast majority of them are not at all harmful (nudge to my arachnophobic younger brother).

Improvisers don't simply let go of the fear of failure; they develop a unique attraction to it. They have a sixth sense for juicy little failures and an excitement around big, meaty failures. In improv comedy, mistakes and failures are our bread and butter. When an improviser says a wrong name, falls, makes a weird voice or anything else accidental, it immediately becomes this phenomenal opportunity for creativity. It's gorgeous!

Most of the books, gurus and success coaches I've encountered encourage people to get over their fear of failure because success is worth the risk. I encourage my students to move past a fear of failure, but in a completely different way. Let's be honest; fear will never fully go away, and failure will always be something we have to come to terms with in our lives.

> Our "failures" and "mistakes" allow us
> to discover gifts for our scenes.

In improv, we aren't just *risking* failure, we are actually aiming for it when we rehearse and embracing it when we perform! We leap without first looking and embrace the result as a gift. Our "failures" and "mistakes" allow us to discover gifts for our scenes. Those are the moments when we surprise and delight ourselves; where genius slips in and new ideas can flourish. It is when we are knocked down that we learn the most about standing up. We play many games that are designed to make us fail as a group and then celebrate the failure as a sign that we stopped trying to be perfect and just "went for it!" These games are so fun and so freeing. This is a very important point worth saying again and again: we stop trying to be perfect.

It's worth repeating because I, in particular, had to learn that over and over again. I grew up being told I could do anything I put my mind to. This was a fantastic gift my parents gave me. I grew up with a fantastic sense of self-esteem and allowed myself to try so many things that I quickly found out what I was particularly talented at and became quite good at those things: soccer, acting, taking tests, and skipping classes without anyone noticing. Two of these skills I still use today.

When I began doing improv, I focused heavily on being "the best." My intention was to be the funniest comedian, the best actor, and the most entertaining performer. I tried so hard to be perfect that I was missing out on much of what improv had to teach me. I played the warm-up games with a competitiveness that went beyond mere fun. I played to never look stupid and to always prove myself the best. My confidence and background in performing usually helped me get away with this.

> After years of being coached in improv,
> I finally learned and incorporated
> the lesson of letting go of control and
> perfection in every moment.

I was someone who rarely admitted I was wrong; and if I was, I didn't deal well with it. So, though I am seemingly bold and courageous and the one who always volunteers first, behind that is a crippling need to be perfect. I desire to be the best and be recognized as such. My therapist helped me realize that being recognized for accomplishments is something important to me and completely valid. It is just one element of what drives me to accomplish so much in my life and is perfectly healthy (did I just say perfectly?!). However, if we judge ourselves on a standard of perfection, we will either not try those things we don't know we are going to be awesome at or will try them and, when we are not perfect, will likely feel terrible about ourselves. No, really, ask my therapist! After years of being coached in improv, I finally learned and incorporated the lesson of letting go of control and perfection in every moment. I became more vulnerable and willing to embrace the moment of "trying" more than the outcome. After all, there are no trophies in improv. For that I am thankful, as I would be obsessed with getting one. Hey, I still like winning!

Elisa is becoming the person she truly wants to be

Have you ever been isolated with just one person? You're so in love with him or her that you spend all your time together. Except that overexposure turns feelings sour. You forget how to connect with people who aren't him or her. When you get out of that sort of relationship, you are completely alone.

That's where improv came in for Elisa. As she puts it, "I'd never been brilliant at connection, but I came out of a meaningful relationship unable to connect with anyone. Unfamiliar social situations gave me panic attacks." A friend of a friend of hers did improv. She had been to one of these shows and, for Elisa, it seemed awful, and relatable, and attractive all at once. She knew the feeling of panic she got when thinking about improv meant there was something about it that would help her find more joy in her life.

It took her four months just to sign up for a free trial class, and another month before she finally signed up for a full class session because, as she puts it, by then she had "forgotten how physically ill the first class made me feel."

She told me she couldn't go anywhere without checking the event or location details two, three, or four times. She had always had social anxiety, but after spending so long relying on someone to guide her through it, she was worse than she had ever been. Unsurprisingly, Elisa was always late to improv class. She rarely participated much. For her, it was exhausting.

She told me her clearest memory of her first class is standing outside the theater, checking that the name on the printed registration form matched the name of the theater. She then checked the receipt on her phone against the receipt she'd printed just in case there was some difference, then checked the class time and address again.

It took immense courage on Elisa's part to take that first step of signing up for class, and then she was faced with the prospect of failure. Walking into the classroom of strangers was well beyond her comfort zone. In her mind, she was certain to fail.

Fortunately, she did enter the classroom and quickly found out that eleven other people in the room were also outside their comfort zone. As Elisa discovered with the support of her classmates, improvisation is a team effort in which we all take risks, big or small, together. Although we feel like these risks might lead to ego-crushing catastrophe, we discover our team has our back, and we cheer and laugh together. Little by little, putting ourselves out there and taking chances to connect with others feels less and less daunting, and more and more exciting.

Elisa did not fully enjoy her first class; it was exhausting for her. But she saw the joy that was possible, so she committed to returning the next week. As the weeks went by, she began to feel less anxious before and during class, and she began leaving class with a smile on her face and joining her classmates for a beer. She is still friends with many of those classmates.

At the same time, Elisa gradually noticed small changes in her life. She started taking risks. She tried things that had always terrified her. She went to a bar by herself. She started hanging out in coffee shops. She invited interesting people to do things with her she had always wanted to try. She even found the courage to leave the job she disliked and get a new job at a company that embraced play and was much more satisfying. For the first time in her life, she started creating real joy for herself instead of just existing.

A year and a half after Elisa faced her fears and put herself in a roomful of strangers playing improv games, I asked Elisa to challenge herself even further by stepping on the stage and auditioning for our house ensemble teams. These teams comprise our best graduates and most experienced improvisers, and they perform in front of packed audiences every week. She had completed all five levels, and many people really enjoyed the authenticity and unique point of view she presented in her student shows. Although the thought of putting herself out there caused great anxiety, she agreed to audition. Because she is a fantastic listener, connects with her scene partner, and allows herself to be vulnerable in every scene, she was picked to join one of our teams. She now rehearses and performs with her team every week. She found a group of friends who are so supportive of each other and have so much fun together they lovingly call each other "siblings."

Elisa says she still has some of the anxiety from "before improv" because it has been strong in her all of her life. She is even amazed that she was confident enough to allow me to share her story. I love how Elisa recognizes that we can never stop embracing our fears if we want to keep growing. Elisa says she is "getting closer to the person I truly want to be every day."

FAIL FAST. FAIL OFTEN

When I talk with students who have been struggling to create a more joyful life for themselves, a common roadblock I discover is that they are trying to make a perfect, fail-proof scenario before they begin making any changes or taking any action. They don't want to seek a publisher until their manuscript is absolutely perfect, or go out on a date unless the person is just what they are looking for. I encourage all of these students to embrace the improv lesson of failing fast and often in their lives.

I encourage students to take a cue from improv and create, do, or be some version of whatever it is that calls to them before they feel ready. I invite them to put it out there for people to see, to declare it, and to notice what was fun about it, or what brought them joy. What was difficult? What was easier than you expected? How did others react?

Before I felt confident enough to be an improv teacher and advertise a public workshop, I invited some friends to let me teach them. I did not feel qualified to be an improv teacher at that point, but I had to begin teaching to become more qualified. I made it clear to my friends that I was just starting out, but I approached the task "as an improv teacher." I jumped in with both feet and found out that I enjoyed it, as did my friends. I discovered where I needed to become stronger as a teacher of improv, and I kept at it.

It is impossible to get feedback before you bring your ideas into the world. Likewise, it is impossible to make something the best without feedback. Sometimes this comes in the form of verbal feedback from those around you, such as users of a product or service, or from trusted advisors. Frequently, the feedback also comes simply from your own results. If your next big thing is to become an athlete, your own body and results will show you what is working and what is not working. My friends told me which parts of the classes they most and least enjoyed, and to this day I learn and improve on every single class I teach based on feedback from my students as well as self-reflection.

These mistakes and failures are crucial because they show us how to be better. I love plans as much as the next person (all right, probably a lot more), but no plan can ever be perfect. In life, we have far too many variables and unknowns. Instead of trying to create a perfect plan, create a prototype and make it real. See how your idea works in this first form, and how it doesn't.

Then, just as quickly, let it go.

Take what you learned from the first version, paying special attention to the parts that didn't work, and make another prototype attempt. Adjust your routine, change your strategy, or tinker with your invention. Then release it all over again, as quickly as you can.

On the stage, improvisers are making constant adjustments based on the reactions of their scene partners and the audience. We try something, see how it works, tweak it, and try again. This is how we learn to be great at what we do, and it's the same process you can use.

Remember that living like an improviser also means practicing the art of letting go. No need to feel bad that your first attempt or first version was not perfect when you were never aiming for perfect.

You aimed to accept whatever outcome happened, and you did. Congratulations! This is step one in achieving a life of joy.

LET'S PLAY! BOO/YAY

The Goal: To get one person to accomplish an unknown task with the direction of the rest of the group

Number of Players: Four to four hundred

How to Play: Ask one person to leave the room. As a group, the others decide on a simple action they will try to get the absent participant to do upon returning. The action can be anything from sitting on a chair to opening a window or interacting with another participant in some way.

We invite the participant back into the room and, as a group, try to get him or her to perform the chosen action. The challenge is that we can only use two words: Boo and Yay! We say Boo to anything that is not what we want the participant to do, and Yay to anything that gets closer to our goal.

Why We Play It: As you can imagine, this is hard. And confusing. People don't like to hear the "Boo," and they don't like to say it. To make matters worse, the first participant to attempt the challenge is often hesitant to try anything because he or she doesn't know what it is he or she is supposed to do. The problem is that if you take no action, it is impossible for your teammates to give you feedback to help you figure out what you are supposed to do.

A common first reaction is to stand still, like a deer in the headlights. This is how most of us react when faced with an unknown course of action. Unlike in Boo/Yay, we often have an idea of what we want to accomplish but no idea how to make it happen. Similarly, we may want to do something great but feel paralyzed because we don't know what our greatness might be. As a result, we stand still, unable to take the leap.

The only way to succeed in Boo/Yay is to simply start doing things. Anything at all will get you closer to your goal, because then your teammates can give you feedback and tell you when you are getting closer. The most successful participants are the ones who attempt as many actions as possible, as fast as possible. These participants get the most information from their ensemble and, as a result, get to their goal the fastest.

Improv is a balancing act between letting go and holding on. We let go of lines that fall flat, moments of poor judgment, and missed opportunities. We hold on to our characters' perspectives, emotions, and relationships. Living like an improviser means taking in everything as a gift, but it also means discarding anything that doesn't serve you. Things like harsh criticism, pessimism, and dwelling on failure are in the category of things that don't serve. Notice all of your thoughts and ideas, but feel completely free to discard the negative ones.

Letting go hinges on accepting this moment exactly as it is. You are equipped with all of your experiences, ideas, and areas of expertise you have acquired up to now. You are not equipped yet with anything you will acquire in the future. This moment is exactly as it is, not exactly how you wish it would be. And it never will be. In all likelihood, no moment will ever be exactly how you would like it to be. Such is the beauty of life; little mistakes and surprises slip in to challenge and inspire our creativity.

If you struggle with simply letting go of the frustrations and the limitations standing between you and your joy, try this: imagine that the limitations are like an obstacle course. Running fifty yards through a straight, flat field is not much of a challenge. It becomes interesting when you must scale a wall, trudge through mud or walk across a balance beam. The obstacles are what make the track interesting and what lead to the feeling of accomplishment at the end. The same can be true of the obstacles in your life; they are what make the road you travel unique. They are what make your story special, and what will make you especially good at what you do when you finally break through them. As improvisers, we turn limitations into challenges that spark our creativity and playfulness.

We learn far more from our mistakes and failings than we do from our successes. A key tenet of improv is that every mistake is a gift. The more mistakes we make, the more gifts we get. This is true in ourselves and in life as well. Try to remember that we are *all* just making this stuff up as we go along. We are all making mistakes. Allow yourself to take more risks, embrace all your mistakes as potential gifts, and cherish every lesson you learn along the way.

> Allow yourself to take more risks, embrace all your mistakes as potential gifts, and cherish every lesson you learn along the way.

Understanding the challenges in our life is crucial to solving them. Our struggles inform and expand our drive to improve. One way to do this is to specifically address what you would like to do differently in order to combat one or more of these facets of yourself or your life that you want to change. For me, it was vulnerability.

When you have no idea where to begin, attempting something is terrifying. I understand how scary it is to take a leap toward the unknown. I can't guarantee your first step will be the right step, but I can guarantee it will be a step in the right direction.

Try something different today. You don't have to know where you are going in order to start. If you know you want something in your life to be different, start anywhere, and change anything. You could start small and switch up what you eat for breakfast or the route you take home from work. You could go bigger and sign up for a class; of course, I recommend improv, but anything that piques your interest is the perfect choice.

It is not so important exactly what you do, only that you do something. Take any action and observe closely how things change and what felt joyful about it. Then take some more action. Keep going.

CHAPTER SUMMARY

▶ Don't wait for the perfect moment or perfect plan; start now.
▶ Mistakes lead to delightful surprises.
▶ Failure breeds success.
▶ Did we mention, start right now? (Really, right now.)

EXPAND YOUR COMFORT ZONE

I have a little dog named Louie. He is a 12-pound miniature pinscher that loves people. He's not much of a barker, except when another dog walks by our front yard. We have a fence around the perimeter of the yard, and when Louie sees a dog on the other side, he runs and barks. Up and down along the fence Louie runs and barks, and there is almost nothing I can do to stop him. He's protecting his territory.

He is within his comfort zone, and he lets every other dog know it is not allowed in. His little yard is his zone of safety. All the other dogs represent a threat to his (our) safety. They are unknown and unwelcome. He has an actual bark to announce that. We all have our own comfort zones; and though we might not bark, we have our own ways of staying safely inside our little yards.

We develop our comfort zone early in life, and the experiences we have help define it. Our comfort zone is there to protect us and help us survive. It serves us very well most of the time, but there are times when our comfort zone can't protect us or help us grow as individuals.

Louie does not enjoy going to the dog park. He loves walks on the leash and going to work with me to see all his human friends, but the dog park is beyond his comfort zone. At the dog park, other dogs rush up to him and sniff him all over. They get in his face (and other areas), and his body language shows that he is uncomfortable and anxious.

> We expand our possibilities for the
> future and are more prepared to deal
> with the unexpected events that are thrown at us.

We all have our own version of Louis's dog park in our lives—and we can stay safe within our little yards, unless we want to grow. Inside our yards the possibilities are limited. Beyond them, who knows?

Every time we try something new, we expand the fence around our yard a little bit more. I've seen hundreds of people do this with improv. For many, the fence is now practically invisible. Through improv we build our capacity to take risks. Over and over again we say, "Why not?!" and we take the next step. Saying "Why not?!" is saying "Yes! And . . ." to ourselves and our ability to try something. We stop panicking and trying to control every situation. We just say "Yes, And . . ." to the reality, and add to it. We're saying, "Bring it on!" and we can use that switch whenever we want to (or have to) step out of our yard.

We start slowly at first, with easy games that help reinforce the feeling of failing without major consequences to our life or our ego. Then we push further. This "why not?!" ability is like a heavy gate on the fence of our yard that gets easier and easier to open each time we try something that makes us uncomfortable. By working this muscle, we expand our possibilities for the future and are more prepared to deal with the unexpected events that are thrown at us. That is why improvisers are known for thinking on their feet. It isn't something we are born with; it is a skill that we practice over and over.

Page learned to trust herself as well as others

Page lived just a couple blocks from the theater and would walk her dog past it on a daily basis. Page lived a mostly solitary existence. She'd go to work and then go home, with little social life. She had had a difficult life with little support from family, had little reason to trust others, and struggled with emotional issues. Most of all, Page had very little faith in herself.

One day she walked in and discovered what we were about. Page thought it might be satisfying to act. She was looking for something she could be good at and use to find more joy in her life. I love that Page even thought about something that seemed in opposition to her life and low self-esteem at the time. Clearly, Page had a great desire in her to do something challenging and creative, and that involved collaborating with others. Ultimately, she wanted to find something she was good at and feel better about herself.

After seeing a show, she started thinking about taking a class. The training center had a flier on the door, and she took one home and taped it to her wall. It took her nine months to work up the courage to enroll in her first class.

Page says her first day of class was well out of her comfort zone but was an incredible experience. Kat Brown was her first teacher. Page says Kat "expressed so much energy, positivity, and support it was impossible not to absorb some of it and begin to imagine a life without the massive self-doubt I always felt." Page felt incredibly awkward and stifled in the beginning, fearful of making a fool of herself. She also felt incredibly vulnerable. However, by the end of the seven-week introductory class, she realized she was learning to let go of some of her self-doubt just by focusing on having fun in the moment and not thinking as much about how people were judging her. She realized that everyone was learning to be less self-critical and focused on playfulness.

That was almost two years ago, and the path to self-discovery and increased self-esteem has been both difficult and extremely rewarding for Page. I have watched as so many people supported her in her journey to believe in herself and allow herself to shine. She has a renewed purpose in life and a supportive community of friends who share that with her.

Knowing that there were times Page felt extremely uncomfortable and frustrated with herself during her beginning months of improv, I asked her why she kept going. She said the improv "bug" bit her somewhere during level two or three. She realized she was beginning to feel moments of joy and eagerness, even a sense of satisfaction with life that had drained out of her years prior. She looked forward to seeing shows, being in class, and being part of a community. She started to care about being present for every moment and recognized that it was safe to trust people again.

Page is now a student in my six-month-long graduate conservatory. When I asked Page what she loves about improv, she explained that for her it is about laughing, playing, creating, interacting, living in the moment, and learning. She is confident in her answers and in herself. Her original goal was to see if acting would be fun for her. Her new goal is to be on a team and eventually to teach improv to others so they can experience more joy in life, like she has.

Improvisation builds courage to make bold choices and take risks. We take chances over and over. When we stand on stage with another improviser, get a suggestion from the audience, and leap into an unknown scene, we have no idea if this will be the best scene or the worst scene we have ever done. But we stepped on stage and trusted that all the practice we've done to that point has prepared us to find value and joy in either outcome.

If our comfort zone is small, we may never step on stage. When my comfort zone for singing was very small, I didn't allow myself to sing in front of others. I missed out on so many opportunities to improve as a singer or simply just enjoy singing for fun. If we never step on stage, we can't create something potentially wonderful. Stepping out on an empty stage in front of an audience will be one of the scariest (and most thrilling) things you can do in life. Even after many years of doing so week after week, my heart rate still rises, and I begin perspiring. And every time, I become more confident, more comfortable, and have more fun. To do so, you have to practice saying, "Why not?!" or you will be stuck standing backstage while everyone else is creating something wonderful onstage.

When we can say "why not?!" more often, we can open the gate and step outside of our yard. And when we get more comfortable with that, we can experience more things in life and find even more joy. Remember, we aren't born this way. As babies we cried our lungs out if our environment changed the least bit. As adults, are we really that much different? Ask yourself how big your comfort zone is. How often do you step outside of it? When was the last time you did something to expand your comfort zone?

If you find it hard to get out to the dog park and wag your tail a bit more, find a group of supportive people you can practice trying new things with.

In improvisation classes, we spend a lot of time building support and trust among each member of the group, so that everyone in it feels comfortable stepping just a little bit outside of his or her usual comfort zone. Each week, everyone's comfort zone grows and grows, and what people are able to do without their ego inhibiting them is mind-blowing. It truly is the quickest way I know to build confidence and be prepared to take on the unexpected.

It's when our minds finally stop panicking and trying to control every situation that we can say "why not?" or "bring it on!" That's when you can step on stage and create something wonderful to bring more joy to your life.

LET'S PLAY! HOT SPOT

The Goal: To "rescue" the person in the middle by tagging them out and starting a new song

Number of Players: Can be played with as few as two people but is best with five or more.

How to Play: To play, stand in a circle with your ensemble. One person stands in the middle and starts singing a song. As soon as anyone on the outside recognizes the song, he or she begins singing along. Don't know the song? Think of other ways to support the center person; clap in rhythm, hum, or dance. As soon as someone in the circle is reminded of another song, that person tags out the center person, takes his or her place, and begins singing.

Why We Play It: This game builds the muscles of putting yourself out there, taking a risk, and letting your ensemble support you.

Improvisers often have a love/hate relationship with this game. When we introduce it, it invokes almost universal terror. "You want me to sing? Alone? In front of people?" The point is not to be a great singer; rather, the point is to support one another to make this kind of awkward thing much less awkward by taking care of each other.

This exercise builds two important skills: Taking risks and trusting your ensemble. Most of the time when we set out to do something great, we have to take a leap and risk failing or—worse (gasp!)—looking stupid. This exercise gets us comfortable taking that risk in a low-stakes environment, so we feel prepared to take bigger risks in our lives.

CHAPTER SUMMARY

▶ Examine your personal comfort zone.

▶ We are in charge of growing our comfort zone.

▶ Improvisation allows us to practice saying "why not?!" so we can expand our comfort zone.

▶ Expanding our comfort zone leads to more possibilities and more joy in our life.

BE MORE AUTHENTIC
AND VULNERABLE

Most people assume improvisation is about being funny. While this is a fair assumption, it is not entirely accurate. We believe that comedy is the byproduct of improv that is done well. In other words, if you use the principles of "Yes! And . . . ," giving gifts and taking risks, you will find that those watching will be engaged and laughing with you.

I often have students who have been told they are very funny; I can tell they are the life of any party and can tell a great joke. Those are the students who sometimes struggle the most when they begin improv. I myself thought I was pretty funny at one point, with my quick wit and biting sarcasm. I certainly got a few chuckles—but I didn't make a lot of authentic relationships that way. My sarcasm was a defense mechanism that kept people interested in the person I was presenting to them, and not the real me.

At Finest City Improv we put a lot of emphasis on teaching people how to let down their guard. We help them connect with others and be more authentic, relatable, and vulnerable versions of themselves instead of trying to make people laugh. When students are able to do this, they find that improv becomes much less work and more fun. They also discover that everyone finds them much funnier and more delightful.

Dave challenged himself to be more vulnerable

Dave is a 38-year-old elementary schoolteacher who works with autistic children. He loves dancing to house music, practices holistic medicine, and meditates every day. He loves improv because he loves being funny, entertaining people, working with others, and challenging himself to learn new things. He is also a big believer in the spiritual evolution it supports, such as helping people be more confident in showing their true selves (being vulnerable) and finding joy in connecting with others.

Dave started improv classes to get over his fear of performing, to challenge himself to learn something new, and to meet new people in order to widen his social network. He says that he enjoyed improv right away; it turned out to be exactly what he was looking for. Improv provides him with a much-needed creative outlet. It gives him a chance to get out of his shell and do something a lot of people may not have the courage to do. It gives him a chance to connect with a group of people and work together to create a scene, a moment, an emotion, etc. He has tried salsa dancing and other things . . . but he thinks improv is the best!

Dave quickly saw how improv positively influenced him outside the classroom. He noticed that he is less nervous in general and particularly when dating. He is now less worried about "being who I am in all ways." His ego has let go a little bit, and he has found the peace that can happen when one stops trying to be perfect. He is less nervous and less focused on being perfect when called on in a workshop or asked to step on stage at a presentation. He now sits in the front rather than hide away in the back of the room.

Dave has become a wonderful performer as well. He is incredibly supportive and fun to play with. I have invited him to be a part of one of our newest shows, "A Single Lady." He is a great asset to the team and the show, and I am thrilled that Dave decided to take a chance on improv.

Dave says he plans to continue to do improv as a sort of "spiritual practice" that challenges him at every level. It helps him "get out of his head" and let go of his egotistical aspects. Improv helps him overcome his fear of being vulnerable and completely seen for who he is and what he has to offer. He agrees that it is challenging at times, but worth it in every way possible!

The value of being authentic and vulnerable is one of the greatest lessons I have learned from improv. I have always identified as a strong, independent woman. I take charge and make things happen, and I love this about myself! Unfortunately, this attitude can make it hard for me to let people help when I need it, accept failure, and create authentic relationships. By embracing the principles of improv, I gained the ability to share my vulnerability with others without letting go of one ounce of strong, independent womanhood.

The willingness to be vulnerable is so important. Only when we let others see our fears do we give them the opportunity to connect with us on a deeper level. As a way of inviting you to be vulnerable with me, I'd like to share something personal with you. Personal stories are riddled with vulnerability, yet telling them also demonstrates our strength because it lets others know of our struggles and our accomplishments.

> The value of being authentic and vulnerable is one of the greatest lessons I have learned from improv.

I am very proud to be an ovarian cancer survivor and can confidently say that much of my strength—and my aversion to vulnerability—are derived directly from that experience. At just 12 years of age, I put on a shield of emotional armor and fought against the cancer that threatened to take me away from my family. I endured many long months of terrible sickness. In reality, the doctors, the surgery, and the radiation fought the cancer. I was fighting against the absolute terror I saw in the faces of everyone around me. They were scared and I was scared—and rightly so. As a result, I "took charge," wearing my suit of kick-ass armor.

Already a confident and "scrappy" girl, I cried little and put on a brave face for everyone around me, especially my parents and younger brother. Heck, I was the girl who, just weeks earlier, had had four teeth pulled to make way for badly needed braces and still insisted on playing my clarinet in a school show that night. So, when everyone around me was frightened, I fought for them all, so they would be assured that I would survive. The only time I remember crying was while the anesthesiologist was counting down as I lay on the operating table. I have trouble identifying a time after that in which I allowed myself to cry in front of others.

It wasn't until about thirty years later that it dawned on me that I was too scared to show the slightest bit of vulnerability! To do that meant to give in to the horrible fate I saw reflected in everyone else's eyes that terrible summer. I spent thirty years continuing to fight or flee from those feelings of vulnerability. As you can imagine, changing up one's "modus operandi" is very difficult when linked to such a traumatic experience. It's why we have therapists! And, as it turns out . . . improv!

The therapist assisted me in naming the trauma and my intense need to be the bravest and "least affected" person in the room. When I imagined myself back in the hospital room as an eighty-five-pound sixth grader, I realized I could have just said that I, too, was scared. I could have let everyone else take on some of the burdens I believed to be all mine. I could just have asked to be hugged. Seems pretty simple now, but just saying those words still leaves me ill at ease, because that is vulnerability. To me, that feels like weakness. But during the summer of '82, that meant the worst result imaginable.

The therapist helped name the issue: vulnerability. But improv classes and practice are where I truly made friends with vulnerability, and I am gradually embracing it as a strength instead of a weakness. I perform with a tremendously talented all-female improv ensemble called Swim Team. One year our team invited a guest coach to work with us. She identified each player's strengths and challenged each of us to try a different way of playing in order to balance out the entire ensemble.

If you haven't guessed already, my strength was my ability to be bold, make strong choices, and take command. My weakness? Not enough vulnerability. Many others on the team were not fully able to contribute because I was so closed off at times. That day, we did a show in which I challenged myself to be "the most vulnerable person in the world," and it was freeing and cathartic—as improv can often be. Best of all, the entire ensemble truly "gelled." We all played so well together, like the team of doctors from my horrible summer fighting cancer at Upstate Medical Center. I let go of my fear and felt tremendous support from the rest of my teammates. That night, we had one of our best shows ever, and I had more fun than ever before.

This was a great reminder that improv is not just about creating funny characters and heightening the antics that make for surprising, delightful comedy. It's also about being honest and raw and vulnerable with others. Most great improv starts from a place of authentic connections. So I have the ability to say whatever is on my mind, which is a great strength. And through hundreds of improv practices and shows, I have been offering a less controlled, less armored version of myself. I am learning to be vulnerable on stage for my ensemble as well as in my life with my colleagues and friends. I am grateful to have this art in which I can practice vulnerability without "real world" consequences. I am letting others "pull weight" and "fight" instead of thinking I have to do it all for everyone.

> Most great improv starts from a place of authentic connections.

Theoretically, we all know we aren't alone and don't have to do it all. Every now and then we are lucky enough to practice it and see it played out in earnest. This reminds me of one of my favorite improv shows I've played in. It was a show with Swim Team, the same team I described earlier. Being a "middle-aged" woman, I am often developing scenes centered on my experiences with relationships, children, reproduction, and women's rights. On this night we did a show whose theme was infertility, and the many struggles and choices that arise out of this: the fear, the sadness, the questions about whether and how to adopt, the way it impacts our relationships—all of the deep, sticky, often icky, too-close-to-home issues. We weren't making stereotypical jokes, goofy choices, or hackneyed one-liners. We explored something real, honest, and personal. And I was vulnerable and played a woman who expressed her fears about ovarian cancer and her struggles with infertility, something I could speak about from the heart quite well. We used comedy in order to open up the space and make room for this very difficult conversation, but in the end comedy really wasn't the point. The point that evening was that we were able to share things that are difficult for us and feel a little less alone in the world.

> We were able to share things that are difficult for us and feel a little less alone in the world.

After the show, a woman from the audience approached me and told me she had had ovarian cancer that left her infertile and so depressed she had not left her home in months. That evening was the first time she went out, and the first time she had laughed since cancer invaded her life. She thanked our whole group for the experience and, of course, we were all moved to tears by the enormity of the connection we had created together. That night will always remind me of the power of improvisational comedy and the ways in which it helps us grow, both on stage as well as off stage.

LET'S PLAY! PORT KEY

The Goal: To share our stories with others in a supportive way

Number of Players: Works best with three to five people.

How to Play: Start with a random word as a suggestion (a starter word or phrase that is your inspiration) such as "tomato" or "short." As soon as the word is voiced, one person in the circle completes the following statement without taking more than a few seconds to think about what he or she is talking about.

"When I think of (suggestion word), I think of _____."

That person keeps talking, sharing a story or anecdote about something that really happened in his or her life or something he or she truly knows about. The goal is to be authentic—even a little vulnerable—and not pre-plan what you will share.

This person continues for about a minute or two and then takes a random word mentioned in his or her anecdote, and offers that as a suggestion to another person in the circle. That person takes the new suggestion, completes the sentence, and shares his or her own story or anecdote based off the new word. This repeats until everyone in the circle has spoken two or three times. While others are talking, no one may interrupt or ask questions. Just listen and be interested in what they are sharing.

Why We Play It: We often feel a lot of pressure to "be interesting" and don't think that we naturally are. When we play this game, we find that everyone has life experiences that are quite interesting to others because we relate to many of them ourselves. When we work hard to invent and embellish the truth, people feel you performing for them and are less interested. This exercise demonstrates the value of authenticity and vulnerability. It also shows us just how much of our lives and our viewpoints are interesting to others without needing to be epic moments. Instead, we love simple moments of truth.

The exercise is called port key because the one-word suggestion, when "handed" to us, instantly takes us in our mind to a time and place that was real for us. We can see and hear it in our minds and bring back the feelings related to that experience. The port key is a magical key that can transport us instantly to a place we don't have to invent. It helps us be real, authentic, and a little more vulnerable.

CHAPTER SUMMARY

▶ Practice being a more authentic, relatable, and vulnerable version of yourself.
▶ By sharing openly, we make meaningful connections with others.

TRUST YOUR ENSEMBLE

A core tenet of improv is that we always have each other's backs. Backstage, right before a show, many improvisers look each other in the eyes, pat each other on the back, and say, "I've got your back!" This level of support allows us to take risks and have more fun on stage. We know that any move we make will be supported by one of our teammates.

> "I've got your back!"

Since I started doing improv, I find myself saying, "I've got your back!" to others all the time. We often have the backs of our friends, family, and colleagues, but we don't always recognize it or say it as clearly as I've experienced with improv teams. In improv, we do this almost every time we go on stage. It makes a huge difference. If this helps create our best team performance on stage, it can certainly help us perform better with others in our daily lives. I think we should do it as often as possible.

When Finest City Improv opened its doors, I thought we would be a lot like the big improv theaters in Los Angeles and Chicago, a place where up-and-coming talent trained for the big stages of the comedy world. While we certainly have had many incredibly talented and hilarious performers grace our stage and classrooms, the vast number of students and guests who come to us with a different story continues to surprise us. "I just got divorced," "I just moved here and I don't know a single person," and "I feel completely stuck in a rut in my career" are equally as common reasons for people to take classes as wanting to be the next Amy Poehler or Will Ferrell. In fact, performing is typically the least common reason for enrolling in our classes.

Group after group of introductory students have found strength from classmates. Many of these groups go through all five levels together and build bonds that last for years. I often hear students and performers say that the people in their group really "get them" and that they trust them implicitly.

Jason found the love of his life!

Improv has a way of bringing together a community of people with whom, anytime you are with them, you are having the best time of your life. When Jason relocated to San Diego, he found himself searching for friends he could relate to. He didn't have much luck until he enrolled in an improv class.

Jason had been involved with improv in his previous community, so he knew that people who do improv were probably the people he wanted to be around. As he relates, "Improvisers say 'Yes!' to the new people in the room, invite them into their circle, and genuinely want to know them.

They are so well-trained in authentic communication that they make truly excellent friends."

Jason joined one of our house teams and also began teaching improv to others. When Jason encountered difficult times at work and with personal issues, he found great strength through his improv family. At least twice a week he knew he would laugh and play and be fully supported by his fellow improvisers, whether in the training room, on the stage, or just out in the lobby before and after shows. Jason became a happier person during his time at Finest City Improv, and one wonderful woman took notice of the joy that he felt and shared with others. He proposed to Christine onstage one day and she said, "Yes! And . . ."

Jason and Christine have since moved to a different city for work, but we keep in touch with them regularly, and many of us attended their wedding.

ENSEMBLE VS. TEAM

In improv, a lot of performing groups refer to themselves as "improv teams," but at Finest City I often refer to them as "ensembles." What's the difference? A team is, with few exceptions, fighting against something or for something. They are people who cooperate in order to win against an opponent or to accomplish a specific goal.

In contrast, an ensemble is a creative and collaborative group. They need no adversary in order to strive for greatness, and their goal is generative, rather than competitive. Ensembles are extremely adept at identifying the strengths and weaknesses of their members and adapting to accommodate. Ultimately, ensembles raise everyone up.

> Ensembles are extremely adept at identifying the strengths and weaknesses of their members and adapting to accommodate. Ultimately, ensembles raise everyone up.

YOUR ENSEMBLE

Just like improv, life is an ensemble activity. Even the most successful, intelligent, and courageous among us could not possibly do it alone. However, you don't have to let just anyone into your ensemble. That choice is up to you.

Finding your ensemble is a crucial step toward finding joy. Not because you are not powerful and creative and wonderful enough all on your own, but because it is impossible to discover the full extent of yourself by yourself.

> Taking big risks is much easier when you have an ensemble you trust to catch you.

Taking big risks is much easier when you have an ensemble you trust to catch you. We use many exercises in improv to build an ensemble within each class and performing group. While the group is building trust, each individual is also developing his or her own ability to let others help him or her. For those of us with an independent "I-can-do-it-all" streak—and I put myself at the top of the list—this can be challenging but extremely rewarding.

LET'S PLAY! 'I LIKE . . .' SEAT SWAP

The Goal: To find commonalities and make connections within a group

Number of Players: Best for five to fourteen people

How to Play: One person stands in the middle of a circle of chairs. There are only enough chairs for those sitting. The goal of the person who is standing is to find commonalities with others so he or she can take a seat. The person in the middle finishes the statement, "I like _____." Anyone who agrees with that statement immediately jumps out of his or her seat and tries to take another open seat. The person who is standing also attempts to take a seat. There is no discussion or comment. Focus on the people who stood up and agreed. The people who remain seated are encouraged not to do or say anything negative. Simply note who has certain things in common.

To take this further, encourage everyone to be much more specific. For example, instead of "I like pizza," say, "I like pizza hot out of a wood-fired oven with fresh tomatoes and goat cheese." Everyone will have to listen all the way to the end of your statement, and you will find who shares more specific interests with you. Furthermore, be agreeable! If you are wavering on whether you agree or not, allow yourself to agree and play!

Why We Play It: This is a super-fun way to share things about yourself and find commonalities without the pressure of justifying yourself. The moment you get your statement out, the competitiveness of the game kicks in, and people don't dwell on your statement. We play this and many other games just like this to find connections within groups and build trust.

YOUR ENSEMBLE AT WORK

Finest City Improv introduces improv to hundreds of company executives and employees each year through our "At Work" program. Most of our clients contact us because they want members of their team to be more creative, more confident, and quicker at thinking on their feet. Before we address any of these skills, we spend quite a bit of time developing their ensemble.

Improv teaches us to trust in our teammates and strive to make everyone look good.

All good teams—and their ability to be creative and confident with each other—are built upon support and trust among the members. Improv teaches us to trust in our teammates and strive to make everyone look good. Improv teaches us to think: "It's not mine, it's *ours.*" Before we go on stage, we look each other in the eyes and say, "I've got your back!"

Companies hire us to help their employees perform with the same level of confidence and creativity we have on stage. What they quickly learn is that what we are able to achieve is primarily because we've spent so much time developing a supportive and trusting ensemble. We teach them that leaders must build and maintain a culture of support and trust within their teams to empower them to perform at their full potential. We teach them to take the time to connect with each other in many different ways outside of their normal routines, and even look each other in the eyes and say, "I've got your back!" Then your work team will feel like a great comedy or jazz ensemble in which all the various talents and strengths will begin to work together to create more wonderful things.

FOR INDEPENDENT ACHIEVERS

Like a lot of high achievers, I always hated group projects when I was in school. I was so concerned about the end result being perfect, and about making myself shine, that I would take on all the work. I assumed that not only could I do it all myself, but that it would be better if I did.

Ultimately, that cycle left me feeling resentful of others for letting me take on so much work, and created a product that was not as strong as it could have been with the benefit of others' input. Improv taught me that creative processes yield much stronger results when we are able to pull the best out of everyone in the group. There is no best idea; rather, there is a best process to generate great ideas.

The great surprise is that utilizing an effective group process actually makes strong performers stand out even more. Achievement and success increase when the group comes together to create something amazing, and in this context, individuals reap more rewards and recognition for their contributions. This is in part because of the superior final product, and in part because when you help draw out and support other members of your ensemble, they are proud to lift you up in return.

LET'S PLAY! QUESTION BALL

The Goal: To explore answers to thought-provoking questions in a safe environment

Number of Players: Two or more

How to Play: Stand in a circle. One person holds an imaginary ball. That person proposes a question to the group. Anyone who wants to answer the question puts his or her hands out to "catch" the ball. Once that person answers the question, he or she looks for other hands ready to "catch" the ball (and also answer the question). Once there are no hands out showing willingness to answer the question, the person holding the imaginary ball proposes a new question.

The game continues like this and should not allow for follow-up questions or further discussion during the game. Save that for after, if you want!

Questions may start simply, then build toward more thought-provoking inquiries. Examples:

▶ Where have you not yet been in your life that you would like to visit?

▶ What activities do you remember most fondly from your childhood?

▶ If you could donate $1 million to a single charity, where would you donate?

▶ What do you wish people noticed about you?

▶ Of the people you know well, whom do you most admire? Why?

▶ Imagine that today is your eightieth birthday. Whom do you hope will be there to honor you, and why?

▶ What is one thing about you that is different from everyone you know?

▶ What is something you like, but don't do often enough?

Why We Play It: We usually play this to build support and trust within groups. The format allows anyone to offer answers without having to provide further justification. Usually, after a few people answer questions authentically, those who have been reticent to share begin to do so. I hope you will find some close friends or family members to play this game with you, and use it to begin clarifying for yourself what inspires you and what guides you.

TAKE THE APPLAUSE. YOU'VE EARNED IT

One of the greatest values of an ensemble is to have champions in your corner with you. When you understand what each other's goals are, you can cheer each other on and celebrate each other's successes.

I have a tradition with my improv groups that when we come off stage after a show, we focus on what we did well. We take just a few minutes to stand in a circle and each say one or two things that were really fun about the show or things that others did that we loved. Just last night I told my fellow teammates that I loved how quickly they supported me as I flopped to the floor. None of us knew why we were on the floor in that moment, but being able to look beside me and see that my scene partner was right there was what mattered most. I felt incredibly supported in whatever risky move I might make.

What we absolutely never do is give each other notes about what we did not like or what we think we did wrong or poorly. We don't criticize each other or ourselves. We are already doing it in our heads, I'm sure, but we don't let it sully the moment, which we deserve to enjoy fully. We just stepped out onto a bare stage in front of an expectant audience and entertained them on the spot for thirty minutes. They applauded us when we were done, and we deserved it. We also deserve to applaud each other and ourselves. Most of all, we deserve to let ourselves enjoy the applause. When we head out to the bar and audience members tell us what a great show it was, even if we thought it was one of our worst yet, we graciously say "thank you" and leave the critical thoughts in our head.

> We deserve to let ourselves enjoy the applause.

This takes practice. It is very easy to "be humble" and say, "Thanks, but I could have been better." We truly are our own worst critics. Why do we feel the need to help others criticize us, too? Do we not believe we could be as entertaining, interesting, or funny as others think we are? Take the applause. Sure, be humble. But be gracious and interested in what their experience was, not yours.

> When you have done something that took courage and someone wants to share the joy you created for them by your actions, please give yourself permission to take the applause in whatever form it appears.

We work on improving the things we did not like about our last show, but we wait until the next practice, and we let it be directed by our coach. The point is, when you have done something that took courage and someone wants to share the joy you created for them by your actions, please give yourself permission to take the applause in whatever form it appears. Do not say "Yes, but . . ." or "No . . ." to that gift. The more you take the applause, the more you build your confidence and believe that what you are accomplishing really is to be applauded.

I've been to many conferences where truly brilliant and accomplished people are introduced as speakers, and the first thing they do is tell us they are not worthy of all the accolades in the introduction. Yes, they are. They wouldn't be at that lectern—and I wouldn't be there to listen—if they weren't. Do not cut yourself down, because we are all cheering for you. We want you to succeed. Sure, there are a lot of insecure people in the world who think it would make them happier if you didn't succeed. Those aren't the people you need in your ensemble. Let them go.

When the spotlight shines on you, show us what you are capable of. And when people applaud you for it, take a bow. You earned it.

IDENTIFY YOUR ENSEMBLE

The ensemble of your life may or may not be one cohesive group, and that's fine. You may find ensemble members in your work life, creative pursuits, hobbies, or amid your family and friends. I hope you will find them in each grouping. The important thing is finding people with whom you can laugh and be exactly who you are in the moment, completely free from judgment. These are the people with whom you feel playful and supported, and whom you can trust completely. These are the people who have your back and celebrate your success.

If this description sounds like something you need more of in your life, I highly recommend taking an introductory improv class. Whether or not you have any interest in ever setting foot on a stage, improv creates these sorts of relationships.

If improv isn't right for you (sometimes it's not, but I have only found a few rare cases where that's true), then take the principles you've learned in this book and apply them to finding your ensemble in a swim club, pottery class, book club, or anywhere that interests you. Just remember to step outside of your comfort zone and say, "Yes! And . . ." to the possibilities as well as to the people whom you meet.

This step is crucial because when you fail, like every one of us does sometimes, you will need your ensemble. You will need the people who have your back unconditionally, will give you the feedback you need and always give the gift of "Yes! And . . ."

CHAPTER SUMMARY

- ▶ An ensemble raises everyone up by identifying skills and filling in for weaknesses.
- ▶ You are amazing, but you cannot do it alone.
- ▶ Your ensemble will catch you when you make mistakes and help you get back up again.
- ▶ A good ensemble will make you a star.
- ▶ When the spotlight shines on you, bask in its glow!
- ▶ You need an ensemble at home, at work, and at play.

DID IMPROV REALLY CHANGE MY LIFE?!

Yes! And it continues to do so every day.

Learning and incorporating the principles of improv into my life has truly made me a happier person. So much so that I spent hundreds of hours writing this book to encourage others to give it a try. I'm still the kid who always volunteers first, but now I am also looking for ways to support others who aren't comfortable raising their hand and standing up in front of others. Now I am less interested in being right and being interesting myself, and more interested in what's interesting about others and what they have to offer. I have let down my guard little by little and allowed myself to become more authentic and vulnerable. Because of improv, I am better at relating to others and can more easily recognize opportunities for fun, laughter, and joy.

My hope is that you will join us at Finest City Improv or at an improv school wherever you live, and begin your own journey of growth and self-improvement centered on quieting your inner critic, developing more courage, connecting more with others, realizing your full potential, and—most of all—discovering more joy in your life! Even if you never step on stage to perform for an audience, you can use these skills to say, "Yes! And . . ." to all the opportunities that pass you by when you aren't confident enough to raise your hand and take a risk on more happiness.

As the stories in this book attest, the hundreds of students who have taken a chance with Finest City Improv have experienced amazing transformations. These students have all made exciting and unexpected changes in their lives because of improv. Almost all of them had a high level of anxiety about taking a class that required them to be vulnerable in front of strangers, to think on their feet, to fail repeatedly, and to trust others. Some of them waited months before taking the first step, even though they knew it would be good for them. For almost every student I've worked with, improv was, at first, well out of his or her comfort zone. And I've seen those comfort zones expand more than the students ever imagined was possible. You can see many of these same students now performing regularly on the Finest City Improv stage or taking elective classes and workshops at our training center to continue to expand their comfort zones, be more creative, and have more fun.

These students have also found an incredible community at Finest City Improv. They have discovered that their true ensemble comprises people who support them in their growth and always have their back. They are the ones willing to look or feel silly at any moment, especially when "failing." They are also the ones who will give you a standing ovation when you succeed.

It's your turn to step forward and discover all that is possible once you take that first step. It's time for you to discover more joy in your life—now! You don't need anyone's permission but your own to take that step. You might trip. You might fall. And I hope you do . . . *repeatedly and spectacularly.* If you don't, how will you discover everything you are capable of?!

Let this be your mantra:

"Yes, I will stumble! And . . . learn something every time I do! Yes, I will be inspired to keeping going forward, loving and trusting the process, whatever the result. And I will discover more joy and laughter in each moment along the way."

By picking up this book you have already said, "Yes!"

What will be your " . . . and?"

COMMON QUESTIONS FROM NEW STUDENTS

When people think about improv a few concerns come up again and again:

ARE YOU GOING TO MAKE ME BARK LIKE A DOG?

People are often concerned that by participating in an improv exercise they'll be asked to do something stupid or make a fool of themselves. While we invite you to shake off the everyday expectations of who you are supposed to be and let a bit of silliness in, our goal—and the goal of every improviser—is to make you—yes, you!—look like an absolute genius. We believe in supporting one another, creating trust and playing to the top of our intelligence. Will you be asked to bark like a dog? Maybe. Will everyone immediately be supporting this together so everyone is having fun and laughing? Absolutely! And then—we will applaud.

DO I HAVE TO BE FUNNY?

Absolutely not! In fact, practicing improv won't necessarily make you a funnier person. Improvisers focus on embodying real characters and exploring genuine relationships. They practice being vulnerable and speaking openly. Very frequently humor comes out of this, often intentionally when it's our goal. But we aren't comedians with one-liner jokes, and you needn't be, either. That said, participating in improv will make you laugh more than ever before and, as a delightful side effect, people may start to identify you as "the funny one."

THERE IS NO WAY I COULD EVER HAVE THE COURAGE TO GET UP ON STAGE AND MAKE SOMETHING UP. DON'T PEOPLE FREEZE/CRY/THROW UP/RUN AWAY?

Sometimes. But that is exactly who this book is for, so why not give it a try? I promise improv will give you all of the tools you need to break through some of your barriers and unleash your potential. You never need to set foot on stage to make this happen, though you may find you want to. I've seen it happen hundreds of times.

CAN I TRY IT WITHOUT COMMITTING TO IT?

At Finest City Improv, we offer monthly two-hour workshops called "Discover Improv" for people who feel that a seven-week class is still too big a commitment. I invite you to sign up for a no-pressure, super-fun, two-hour class that will introduce you to our teachers, other students, and the fun and supportive experience of an improv class. If you are not in San Diego, call your local improv theater and ask about a similar program. Learn more at www.finestcityimprov.com/relax

RELAX SOME MORE:
SEVEN MORE STORIES OF REAL PEOPLE MAKING STUFF UP TO CREATE MORE JOY IN THEIR LIVES

Nixon now uses humor to connect with others

Nixon is a 47-year-old programmer who came to improv because he was dabbling in hypnosis as a hobby and wanted to be better at connecting with people and public speaking. One of his hypnosis instructors recommended improv as a way to practice connection, and a speech club he had joined had an improv demo one night.

Nixon says his first few sessions of improv were "rough." In his first student/teacher show, he froze. I remember working with Nixon in the beginning to help coax him out of his shell. He is now in my graduate conservatory and still struggles with freezing up now and then when he doubts himself. He has learned to accept these moments and now can usually find a way around them, whereas before he was unable to move forward.

Nixon has been practicing improv with Finest City Improv for over a year. Now Nixon finds it much easier to talk in front of groups and with individuals. Before improv, if he knew a social event was coming up, he would obsess about what he would do or say. He would start planning "what-if" scenarios. He says he has stopped doing that. It wasn't even a conscious choice to plan or not to plan; he just doesn't think about it anymore.

He shared a proud moment with me in which his improv training helped him use humor to lighten the mood at a speech club meeting. He was leading the meeting and he knew one person attending was interested in joining the club but had not filled out the needed forms. Since they were friends, Nixon thanked all of the guests for attending and then thanked the group's "undocumented member" as well. That got a laugh from the audience and, immediately following the meeting, the individual he was referring to got the forms together. Nixon says he wouldn't have felt comfortable making that move before improv.

Nixon is now considering trying his hand at stage hypnosis. He says that being connected to the subjects on stage and being able to deal with the unexpected are very important for this, and he feels confident in his ability to do that.

Claire is living a "Yes! And . . ." life

Claire considers herself "an extroverted introvert." She is in a high-profile and high-stress job in the nonprofit world. She signed up for an improv class to find a way to be more comfortable—or rather, less miserable—when put on the spot, which happens to her all the time. She considered Toastmasters but didn't want to learn to give speeches. She wanted to learn how to think on her feet, to be mentally agile, to be affirming, collaborative, and confident—all at the same time!

Thinking of her comic heroes/actors/authors Amy Poehler and Tina Fey, she knew that in addition to being feminists, having great style, class, and being extremely funny, they did improv. She listened to every audio book and podcast and read every article she could find, and both women talked about how foundational improv was to their careers—and their lives. She decided that was also what she wanted!

At first, Claire was very nervous, which she says surprised anyone who knew her. "You're so outgoing!" they said to her. But as Claire was discovering, it is not always the most outgoing person who succeeds in improv. In fact, the greatest lessons she learned were to scale back, don't talk over her partners, and be patient. She also learned quickly that the dynamics required a clean slate, personality-wise. If you're a steamroller, you're going to be very unpopular in improv, because that goes against "Yes! And . . ."

Claire loves the "Yes! And . . ." philosophy she learned from improvisation because it is so positive and supportive. In her words, "It is like, 'of course I will do that for you; what else can I do?'" She sees this as the embodiment of community service. Claire especially loves that the best improv is based entirely on truth, and that it has made her a problem solver and a "kick-ass collaborator."

Improv has improved Claire's personal and professional life in many ways, most of which she never expected. She learned how to really listen and to trust strangers in a collaborative environment. She learned that there are many ways to the same destination, and everyone is entitled to design his or her own route. She learned to go on the journey with her partner, her classmates, and her teachers. She learned to worry less about the outcomes, aka punch lines, and enjoy the journey more.

Claire has learned so much about her true self versus who she thought she was meant to be. She thought she wanted to ham it up on stage in front an audience, but soon learned that her strength and her talent lie in collaboration and support, and that she doesn't need to be the star of the show. "I just really enjoy squeezing every drop out of every moment. Learning how to be in the moment was the biggest gift from taking improv because if your mind wanders while you're doing improv, you are f***ked!"

"Yes! And . . ." has become Claire's personal motto. She truly feels that once she adopted this mind-set, doors began opening for her at work and in her creative life. She says, "It's about being open and receptive to what's going on around you. If you blink, you might miss something really great."

Ben loves to push his boundaries

Ben is a large, imposing man full of kindness and curiosity. He's never been shy and enjoys pushing himself in karaoke to perform songs that are just outside his range. He loves improv because of the amazing people he meets, the challenge of facing fears, and the opportunity to expand his view of the world and how others see it. He also loves the beauty and the sadness of creating unique moments in time that will never exist again.

Ben is the type of person who sees an improv show and says, "Why not?!" to trying it himself. He says he was too scared in college to do theater (though he wanted to), so he took a chance on improv. Ben generally drives himself into new challenges, enjoys seeing how far he can go with them, and responds with, "What can I create?" His first few sessions were a lot of fun. He took the class with one of his best friends, which helped both of them. After the first few weeks, improv started to take up a larger space in his life. Ben never doubted his decision to try improv in the beginning, but as time went on he doubted himself at least once a month. He started to struggle a bit around Level Three and Level Four, as he questioned his abilities. He gained a lot of confidence once he developed more trust in his scene partners and relied less on his well-tuned sarcastic wit. Ben was always funny and confident, but now he is even more so.

Ben says he has always been interested in artistic expression but has had "a peaks and valleys" relationship with the arts in different forms. Choir as a child; drawing and photography in high school; writing, art and philosophy in college; drawing and writing in grad school. He was a bouncer while attending graduate school and says he sometimes adopted a different personality while working the door. He would see how he could use that personality to interact with people differently.

During valleys or dry periods, he did not do anything he considers artistic. He told me a story about studying for oral exams in graduate school. For this, he sat down and studied and memorized for eight to ten hours a day for a month. Any question from his 1,300-page biology book and his research was fair game, so he memorized the entire book. He had the most comprehensive view of the world through science he would ever have.

When he finished this feat, he was happy with this accomplishment but immeasurably sad in other ways. "You could ask me any question in biology, and I had it. But ask me anything outside of science, and I felt dumb as a post. My brain felt like it had shut down. It was the weirdest feeling to have thoughts and not be able to express them. My answers to questions were delayed by twenty seconds, and my friends would just laugh and, of course, take advantage of this. A few nights after my oral exam, I grabbed a fantasy/sci-fi book and started to read. After a period of time it was like a glass protective layer shattered in my head, and all these thoughts flooded into my mind. I knew then that my mind needed artistic expression to function and, more importantly, to be whole." Ben understands now how important this artistic side of him is to his happiness. Improv has become a way for him to express his artistic side and improve himself in many ways.

Ben's life has been defined by pushing boundaries. Setting goals, achieving goals, and pushing some more. Acting is his next goal, and improv is a logical step to reach it. Ben believes that if one can master improv (as much as anyone ever can), then a transition to acting will be easier. As Ben told me, he didn't know how to become a marine biologist, computer engineer, business owner, or politician, but for each of these he set a big, challenging goal and blundered forward. Just like improv, his life is a continuous work in progress.

Christina found a place to fit in with others

Christina is a thirty-year-old who enjoys stand-up comedy, singing in a choir, and "nerding out over coffee." She loves the adrenaline rush and laughter of improvisation as well as the team camaraderie, something she didn't find with stand-up comedy.

Christina loved theater when she was young, but when she went to college, she essentially dropped all things in her life that she deemed impractical. Thus began a decade of her life without the stage. She had a nagging feeling that something was missing. She says her life just "seemed a bit empty." In 2014, she joined a chorus, which she still sings in. She also started going to comedy shows around town and began thinking, "I could do that." She gave stand-up comedy a try and says she "bombed and then did well, and then really bombed."

She had heard that improv was a great skill for comedy. She had had a little improv experience in high school, but didn't have pleasant memories of that experience. Regardless, she decided that the only way forward was to try it again. Now Christina says, "I cannot describe how much it has meant to me to be a part of this community. Improv is where the *weirdos* go." She means that in the nicest way, of course, explaining that it's "where people can go to just be their true selves, whatever that may be." The Finest City Improv community is incredibly supportive, and Christina has found her happy place within it.

Christina has always been a creative individual; she just stopped having an adequate outlet as she "grew up" after college. Even with the courage to try stand-up and improv, she still felt vulnerable and nervous about her first classes, especially because her high school experience wasn't so favorable. However, she says that Level One was like a "love bubble because we were *all* so vulnerable and *all* strangers." Her instructor Shawn was incredibly welcoming and certain to place a metaphorical cushion under anything students might view as a mistake, which is the best kind of introduction/reintroduction to improv anyone can have because you will make "mistakes" constantly!

In her daily life, Christina is sort of reserved, and she holds back a bit if she doesn't know someone very well. But her "improviser self," as she puts it, is purely "her." Meaning, the art that you create and explore onstage is self-exploration; you are exploring yourself and letting everyone else watch you do it without almost no judgment or self-censorship. It really does not get more vulnerable than that. Improvising is Christina's version of opening up to people at an accelerated pace.

Like many people, Christina didn't think much about going through all the levels but now wonders why she would ever stop. She says "I would wither without my weekly session of laughter and community." She is now in Level Four, is a regular at shows and jam sessions, and is beginning to form an improv team with some of her classmates.

Sofia overcame extreme anxiety by learning improvisation

Sofia, 36, grew up in Monterrey, Mexico; lived in Montréal, Canada; and then moved to San Diego a few years ago. Her first language is Spanish, her second is French and her third, still in progress, is English. But that doesn't hold her back from being a wonderful addition to our student community.

Sofia had an intense fear of driving that began after a horrible car accident she had in 2004, when she was learning how to drive. Sofia could not even be in a car for a while, then she started getting in cars but not driving and was always quite anxious in them. So she decided never to learn how to drive.

One morning during her time as a Level One student in our classes, she found herself thinking, "I got this; I can do it" about driving, which is exactly the same thing she would say before doing improv. So she studied for the written test one weekend and passed it. Without thinking too much about it, she called a driving school and took the next step toward her driver's license. At every class she would say to herself, "For the next two hours . . . I got this!" Finally, she made an appointment and passed her driving test on the very first attempt. Sofia was extremely happy and proud of herself. She came to the theater and shared her fantastic news with everyone. She fully attributes her success in overcoming this obstacle in her life to what she developed in improv class. She says that improv awakened a great amount of confidence in herself. She is already planning to go parachuting as her next big challenge!

Han-Ying found friends in a super-genuine and friendly atmosphere

Han-Ying is a 33-year-old who will randomly break out into dance no matter where she is. She moved to San Diego about two years ago. She couldn't find a job as a mental health counselor due to different state requirements. So she was babysitting for a while and realized she desperately needed to meet people and have adult conversations.

She found Finest City Improv on Google, and decided to go watch a show. She admits that, "Honestly, I didn't enjoy the show that day very much because not all the teams were super-funny that night. I said to myself, OK, it's not that hard; evidently I don't have to be funny all the time to be on stage." So Han-Ying signed up for Level One.

Her Level One class was with Kat, whom she describes as "really, truly amazing. Her energy could always reach out to me, and I always felt welcomed and guaranteed to have a good time. I think everyone in the class also felt that way, and this super-genuine, friendly atmosphere helped me to be able to make more friends."

Han-Ying knew that improv was helping her in her life after one of her class performances felt really fun. Everyone onstage had a good time, and the audience laughed and applauded during the show. Her group had only been doing this for a few months, but she says the team was a success because "all of us let go of our lives off the stage and were just with our partners in the moment."

Han-Ying knew how to go to a party and make small talk with strangers. However, after a few months of improv classes, she says she felt more comfortable talking to people in a casual setting. She can now listen to people and participate in interesting conversations. She doesn't think she is a master of social situations, but she can see herself being more confident and can "just be me."

Five things Han-Ying loves about improv are:

1. The people she meets through improv are genuine and honest.
2. Like everything in life, funny or not, she learns from the experience and does better next time.
3. It helps her always be focused in the moment and aware of the team.
4. It challenges her to do things even when she doesn't feel ready.
5. Improv helps her be more confident.

Han-Ying graduated from the core FCI improv program. However, for her the practice and training will never end. She says she will keep taking classes and watching shows. Also, she plans to form or be a part of a team or two and continue her improv life. She is always excited to tell people about improv and invite them to see shows and take classes because she has had so much fun since she joined the improv community. Han-Ying loves to encourage others to join her in this wonderful experience.

Niki matured into a stronger woman

At 24, Niki works for a nonprofit and wants to make a difference in the world, particularly in developing countries and women's development. She also collects rubber ducks and admits to not having watched *Sex and the City* until 2016!

Niki loves the improv community because "everyone is so supportive and willing to share ideas and talk." Niki has found her closest friends in the improv community. She is confident that the lessons she learned in improv double as life lessons. She says she learned so much about herself and how she views the world through improv. Specifically, she is learning to accept uncertainty, which is extremely challenging for her. Because of improv, she is more comfortable living in the moment, being honest and vulnerable, and not needing to know the outcome of something to begin it. Niki has come to believe that the "Yes! And . . ." principle of improv is a phenomenal way to live life.

Niki started taking improv classes because she was new to San Diego, right out of college. Her boyfriend at the time was an improviser and loved it, so they tried it out in San Diego together. They didn't know anyone in San Diego and wanted to make new friends. The transition from college to the real world can often be daunting, especially in a new city, so improv helped her through that super-rough transition and the start of her "adult life." It helped her figure out how to make the best choices for herself, and it taught her the importance of honesty, both to herself and others. Niki says she also tried Meetups to make new friends, but the interactions felt fake to her, and she was uncomfortable at the meetings. She clicked so well with the people in the improv community because, she says, "improvisers tend to have the same values as me or look at life in a similar way."

Niki's first few improv sessions were "a whirlwind of fun, embarrassment, and growth." Her Level One teacher, Shawn, did a great job of presenting improv in a way that made it comfortable for her.

As she continued learning, there were tons of moments when she doubted herself. She would do a scene and tell herself it was awful, so she would go home and think, "Maybe this just isn't my thing, and maybe I'll try something else." However, she kept coming back because she loved the people in her classes, her instructors, and the community. They offered her support and showed her it was OK to fail. She knew she was growing and that we all go through times where our improv feels terrible. She surprised herself, too. One day she would feel like a terrible improviser, and then in the next class she would make a really strong choice. As Niki puts it, "It's a constant up and down, just like life! You've got to fail before you can succeed."

Niki knew that improv was more than just a fun class and that it was affecting her life about six months into training. She realized that because of improv training, she said yes to something she would normally have turned down because of fear. She decided to go to a party where she knew absolutely no one except the friend who invited her. It turned out to be a really enjoyable party. Usually at large parties Niki would get kind of quiet and keep to herself, but at this party she felt so much more comfortable because she could be herself without worrying about how she was being perceived. She ended up meeting someone she considers one of her best friends now, and he introduced her to even more people. She has never regretted saying yes to that potentially awful situation.

Niki has truly seen herself grow more and more into the person she wants to become. She is much more comfortable speaking in front of people, meeting new people, and networking at work. She is more her "true self" because improv helped her connect with her most authentic thoughts, fears, and desires.

When Niki started improv at age 22, she was "young and kind of shy." She wasn't very confident, and she wouldn't make strong choices. She cared a lot about what other people thought about her. Slowly, she started to realize the importance of making bold choices, sticking to your point of view, and letting go of things that do not serve you. These were things she was taught to do in improv scenes, but they also were things she started to do in real life.

Niki clearly remembers one improv class where the guest instructor asked her if she tended to play the submissive character often. Her answer was that she tried not to, but ended up doing it a lot. The instructor told her very clearly to stop doing that because she is "a bad-ass woman and can express your opinions and not let people walk all over you." That hit Niki like a bolt of lightning. Not being submissive is something she had gone to therapists for, and she says it didn't truly sink in until the moment that instructor corrected her and told her to "f**king stand up for yourself." This change was huge for Niki. She says it's something she is still working on, but now she does stand up for herself more, which 22-year old Niki would probably not have done.

RESOURCES & NEXT STEPS

Relax, you finished the book!
When you are ready to learn more or try a class,
visit www.finestcityimprov.com/relax to

- ▶ Connect with me and learn more about Finest City Improv
- ▶ See video clips of some of our performances
- ▶ See videos of the people you read about in this book
- ▶ Find out how to bring improv to your company
- ▶ Sign up to receive monthly tips, exercises and additional stories about using improvisation as a means to create more courage and joy in your life
- ▶ Share your story of how improvisation has brought joy to your life

I hope you are ready to try improvisation. If you live in San Diego, please visit www.finestcityimprov.com/relax to get started. Mention that you learned about us in this book and we'll give you 15 percent off your Introductory Class! Enter code: MAKINGSTUFF UP! (valid through 12/31/2017)

If you don't live in San Diego, check out the webpage for help connecting to our friends, who run great improv schools and theaters in cities all over the country!

ABOUT THE AUTHOR

Amy Lisewski is the Founder and Artistic Director of Finest City Improv. She has over twenty-five years of experience in business and the arts. She is a graduate of the Second City Conservatory and has trained with dozens of top improv teachers from all over the country.

With a master's in library and information science, she helped biotech and high-tech companies improve their internal communications for over 14 years before opening FCI. As a former librarian and alumna of Teach For America, she is dedicated to creating opportunities for lifelong learning.

She travels the country as a Vistage speaker to demonstrate how CEOs and key executives can use the principles of improvisation to improve their leadership skills. She loves the stage and seems to find one wherever she is. She is also a foster mother and an avid sailor, taking risks at home and at sea.

ABOUT FINEST CITY IMPROV

FINEST CITY IMPROV was founded in 2011 as a way to entertain, inspire and bring joy and laughter to the community of

San Diego. For performers and students, loyal fans and first-time visitors, the area's leading improv theater promises a playful and return-worthy experience. More joy. Guaranteed.

Located in the community of North Park, the Finest City Improv stage hosts the largest variety of improvised comedy and sketch shows south of Los Angeles every Thursday through Sunday night. An experienced and dedicated team of instructors teaches improv classes for beginner to advanced students. Finest City Improv also boasts a bold and engaging corporate training program that improves leadership skills, creates stronger teams, and fosters innovation. Find a show, sign up for a class, or schedule your corporate training at www.finestcityimprov.com/relax.